THE MORAL AMBIGUITY OF AMERICA

Paul Goodman

Also by
Paul Goodman

Non-Fiction

The Structure of Literature
Growing Up Absurd: Problems of Youth in the Organized
System
The Community of Scholars
New Reformation: Notes of a Neolithic Conservative
Speaking and Language: Defence of Poetry
Drawing the Line: Political Essays
Decentralizing Power: Paul Goodman's Social Criticism
Format and Anxiety: Paul Goodman Critiques the Media

Fiction

The Grand Piano; or, The Almanac of Alienation
The State of Nature
The Break-Up of Our Camp and Other Stories
The Dead of Spring
Parents' Day
The Empire City

Poetry & Plays

Stop-Light: Five Dance Poems
Three Plays: The Young Disciple, Faustina, Jonah
Hawkweed: Poems
Tragedy & Comedy: Four Cubist Plays
Collected Poems

THE MORAL AMBIGUITY OF AMERICA

Paul Goodman

With an Introduction
by Gilbert McInnis

InExile Publications
Quebec, Canada

National Library of Canada Cataloguing in Publication
Goodman, Paul (1911-1972)

The Moral Ambiguity of America / Paul Goodman
American Culture

Includes bibliographical references.
ISBN 978-0-9876759-1-0
1. American Politics, American History, American Culture.

Printed in Canada for InExile Publications
19 Church St, Sherbrooke, J1M 1S8, Quebec, Canada.
Typesetting & Cover Design: InExile Design

Cover Illustrations: Salvadore Dali, Paranoiac-Critical Solitude, 1935.
Private Collection. Christie's Colour Library, London. DEMART PRO
ARTE B.V./DACS, London, 1990.

CONTENTS

INTRODUCTION
Gilbert McInnis

Paul Goodman's *The Moral Ambiguity of America* went through four editions within four years of its first printing. Just recently (July 2011) the Canadian Broadcasting Corporation decided to podcast his 1966 lecture series.[1] This autumn a film documentary on Paul Goodman, *Paul Goodman Changed My Life* was released by Jonathan Lee. The caption on the front cover (like this book) reads: "The Most Influential Man You've Never Heard Of." This statement may be true of many Americans, but not with the surmountable of interest these days in Paul Goodman's ideas, from students, activists, and grass-root journalists around the world, who are quoting him on the frontlines of their protest activities. The "Occupy Zucotti Park" movement is a case in point.[2] Likewise, Paul Goodman's ideas expressed in *The Moral Ambiguity of America* are not only pertinent for today, they are crucial for our times because Goodman's book documents in detail the practical applications of his activists ideals, and describes through case examples (from over 150 campus lectures) of how his ideas were implemented by various student groups across America.

The Moral Ambiguity of America is a very insightful book to read because it documents Goodman's style of activism during one of the most revolutionary periods of America's history, yet the book provides scholarly reasons for the unforeseeable ambiguity which began in that era of the student movement of the 1960s and prevails

---

[1] The *Moral Ambiguity of America* represents the text of the sixth annual series of Massey Lectures as broadcast on radio during the fall of 1966. The series was arranged by Robert McCormack and produced by Del Mackenzie of the Canadian Broadcast Corporation Department of Public Affairs.

[2] Horatio Morpurgo expressed this in his article about the Occupy LSX event in London, where hundreds of students were arrested outside St. Paul's Cathedral, attempting to Occupy Patenoster Square. Morpurgo also published dates the film on Paul Goodman was to be presented on various campuses across the UK, such as Magdalene College, Goldsmith College, and the University of Sussex. Published on Permalink, November 11, 2011.

today. Likewise, the book offers practical insights into possible recurring ambiguities that might happen again in the world-wide protest movements of today. Hence, *The Moral Ambiguity of America* is a helpful guide for a new generation of "active" citizens who feel the "system" has failed them and therefore pragmatic solutions are needed to approach the current unresolved issues of our times.

Paul Goodman was a passionate activists, and as we read through the pages of this book, Goodman's accounts show us that the heartbeat of the Civil Rights movement did not arise out of the student "mass" movement, but it came from the small "radical student" groups fighting an over-centralized government bureaucracy and from the black American community's struggle to resolve long-standing issues that can be traced back as far as slavery. Hence, in this chaotic environment, we observe how a "majority" fails to live up to the ideals of democratic populism, and therefore, the hope for "change" is left to a small minority instead. Likewise, Goodman offers a generous critique about why his own government failed to resolve these societal conflicts, instead furthering a relationship with a small elite of corporate America which relied heavily on the scientific establishment to "progress" their materialistic agenda of consumerism. All this while the "Republic" tried to maintain its democratic ideals in the face of these two movements and win the wider America over to its new economic program.

Yet, Goodman does not leave his readers to suffer in a hopeless world of cynicism because he attempts to free us from this disempowering "ambiguous" force. Hence, *The Moral Ambiguity of America* pursues (you could say in three sections) societal problems in America and the student response, Corporate America's reliance on technology without much of a moral concern for the implications, and finally, to resolve these concerns, Goodman concludes that Americans must exercise that borrowed Enlightenment idea of "freedom," which those earlier American revolutionaries entrenched in the Declaration of Independence, so they can pursue a "decentralized" system, or else American democracy will not be "viable."

While Goodman's *Growing Up Absurd: Problems of Youth in the Organized System* introduced Goodman successfully to hundreds of thousands of students in America, and perhaps millions, *The Moral Ambiguity of America* provides insightful case examples from Goodman's activism in the 1960s, and more specifically, the book documents how his activism helped students across the nation. For instance, on the vital issue of "decentralizing" for Goodman, we read that "...on 150 campuses I have urged students to work on such problems, in business and engineering, education and communications, science and municipal administration."[3] According to Honeywell, the notion of decentralization is key to understanding Paul Goodman's philosophy:

> For Goodman, centralisation was related to over-capitalisation, mass-consumption, mass-democracy, and mass-education. It was also the cause of modern rootlessness and helplessness, failing democracies, inefficiency and waste. Decentralisation, on the other hand, he argued, created the environment for the human organism to develop selfhood and autonomy.[...] In fact, the term "decentralization" in Goodman's writing seemed to stand as a synonym for anarchism [...].[4]

In *The Moral Ambiguity of America* Goodman provides many case examples that illustrate his notion of decentralization, and how many students he was able to reach and convince "applied it with a lot of energy and some inventiveness" when they created "parallel development" projects (35). These students set up dozens of little 'free universities' in or next to established institutions in order to "teach in a more personal way and to deal with contemporary subjects" (35).

Also, his notion of decentralization was applied by the Associated Students (who also hired him) at the San Francisco State College, which represented 15 000 students. Goodman says that

---

[3] *The Moral Ambiguity of America*, p.34. All other citations hereafter from the book will be cited in parenthesis.
[4] Carrissa Honeywell, "Paul Goodman: Finding an Audience for Anarchism in 20th Century America." (pp. 15-16). Taken from Dr. Honeywell's web page at: http://www.shu.ac.uk/research/spp/sp_carissa_honeywell.html (11/20/11).

the Associated Students have $300 000 annually in student dues [...] which they use for untraditional purposes including organizing a tenants' organization, helping delinquents in a reformatory, running a tutorial program for Black American and Mexican children (with 300 collegian tutors), sponsoring a weekly television program, running an 'experimental college' with twenty offbeat courses, and hiring their own professor. (24)

Likewise, students approached him for help when they wanted to spread his activist ideas with other students on their campuses, usually through their student-run news media. We recognize this as he praises the innovation of these students: "Or consider the college press, with its fairly captive audience of several million, often daily [...] Last winter I wrote a fortnightly column on student matters for a tiny college in Vermont, which the enterprising editor at once syndicated to fifty other college papers" (25).

Nevertheless, Goodman's central purpose throughout the text of *The Moral Ambiguity of America* is not to toot his horn about his involvement in these movements; I only referred to these examples in order to make my case in point about his practical involvement, and to show, at least on the issue of civil rights, how he was happy to praise these students for their convictions. Goodman's illustrations, on the other had, also reveal that the heartbeat of the Civil Rights movement did not arise out of the student "mass" movement, but contrary to popular belief, it came from the small "radical student" groups and from the black American communities. Hence, for an audience today, this book also helps to dispel a long held belief (and myth): that millions of student back in the 1960s were somehow implicated in the civil rights or liberation of the oppressed groups. According to Goodman, this is not the case. Hence, Goodman's insights into the lives of those students who were actually involved with "change" can serve as valuable lessons for today's protest movements, whether in New York, the United Kingdom, or around the world.[5]

---

[5] At the time of writing this Introduction (December 2011), there are over 200 countries represented in the Occupy movement.

Goodman's analysis of the motives of each of the two camps (the "mass" movements versus the radical student groups along with the black American movement) reveals an element of ambiguity on the side of the "mass" movement, and which prevented them from contributing to the advancement of a democratic society. This ambiguity, unravelled, shows insights about a collective and its quest to fulfil its own existential need of finding meaning in an "absurd" world. Goodman says of the "mass" student movement:

> We must remember that these are the young of the affluent society, used to a high standard of living and confident that, if and when they want, they can fit in and make good money. Having suffered little pressure of insecurity, they have little psychological need to climb; just as, coming from impeccably respectable homes, they feel no disgrace about sitting a few nights in jail. By confidence they are aristocrats–en masse. (27)

Goodman also mentions that these students "en masse" imitated the behaviour of the "Voluntary Poverty of the Beat movement, signifying withdrawal from the trap of the affluent economy." Therefore, these "Beat-aristocrats" quested after meaning for their own individual "self," rather than working to change the "centralized" system, and this is why Goodman calls their poverty "voluntary." Likewise, these students did not come from an oppressed class, but from an affluent class, even from Harvard University when "Last year [1965] at Harvard more seniors opted for the Peace Corps than for business (31). In contrast, the only time these affluent students experienced the harsher tone of "involuntary poverty" happened when they visited their black American or Spanish American friends in their respective neighbourhoods (27).

Drawing from his experience with those student movements, Goodman came to the conclusion that change actually happened because of the small radical student groups and the black American community. In contrast to the "Beat-aristocrats," their causes were not necessarily concerned with an existential quest to find meaning in an absurd world, but instead these marginalized activists were fighting for something larger than themselves: the well-being of their families and communities. Between the two camps (radical students and blacks), Goodman supposes that the fervour of that period arose mostly from blacks. For example, he says, "The most spectacular battle with American business-as-usual-and-more-so has been, of course, the belated movement for black emancipation" (21). And history has proven him right.

In addition, Goodman insightfully recognized that the success of the black community to fight racism and especially poverty came about because of the support of their church organizations. Likewise, *The Moral Ambiguity of America* has a lesson for church organizations[6] of today which might be looking to bring back those millions of non-attending, but believing, citizens who have lost faith in a church that has little social application. In contrast, Goodman states:

> There is a revival in the churches. Long pillars of the establishment, they too have begun to take alarm that the establishment is becoming anti-human [...] The churches have latched onto non-directive community-development. Some of them have sponsored the most daring, and unofficious, protest organizations and legal defense for black Americans and Spanish-Americans.(20)

Hence, according to Goodman's report, the churches were reviving, and recognizing that government and its affiliate organizations have become "anti-human." In response, these churches inspired community-development," and some of them even sponsored "legal defense" for those living in extreme poverty.

To return to the "radical students," their activism was not fueled by an individualistic existential need; instead, these students sacrificially reached out to help their fellow humans. In Goodman's words: "Mainly, instead of working in their own bailiwick, the radical students have sought participatory democracy for poor people, organizing rent strikes, marching for black American suffrage, opposing the welfare bureaucrats, and so forth." (32) Yet,

---

[6] A good example here is how the Occupy LSX Movement outside St. Paul's Cathedral, which the London Stock Exchange is immediately next to, was forced to leave by City Council Order. However, The Canon Chancellor of St Paul's Cathedral, the Rev. Dr Giles Fraser, resigned in protest (The Guardian, 27 October 2011).

like the "Beat-aristocrats" these radical students are not necessarily from a disadvantaged class:

> More important, unlike the black Americans, the radical young are not only the middle-class collegians, graduate students, or graduates, but they are also disproportionately the best students and from the best schools. They are an economic force, looming large among the indispensable inheritors of the dominant power in society.(23)

In Chapters One and Two of *The Moral Ambiguity of America*, Goodman documents at length his understanding of these activists, and his illustrations show how they resolved their own societal problems, while at the same time, Goodman provides an analysis of what led to the ambiguity behind these two different student protest movements. Furthermore, the first section of the book narrates his own personal involvement in these movements, and what I particularly enjoyed about this section is how his experience during this period helps dispel the prevailing myth that the sixties protest movements were inspired and organized by the drug culture of "hippies" or a "flower-power" generation. These movements were not central to the change happening in the civil rights movement. Change came about through radical students and the black American community, who had a heart-felt desire to make a better living environment for their communities, not themselves.

In the middle section of the book, chapters three and four, Goodman explores his notion of American ambiguity at another level: his own government's ambiguous relationship with Corporate America, and its reliance on the scientific establishment to implement a "progressive" program of consumerism. Likewise, this "progress" happens as growing urbanization maximizes networks of concentrated people so products can be brought to them with little capital involved. Hence, urbanization and consumerism are essential bedfellows for this progress, and Goodman's chapter "Urbanization and Rural Reconstruction" not only exposes the disastrous results of this progress, but deconstructs the power behind such a model by claiming that rural reconstruction is contrary to it. If we follow the implications to Goodman's view, rural reconstruction is contrary to urbanization because urbanization maximizes networks of concentrated people for the purpose of consumerism, where as rural areas are dispersed and less reliant on consumer products.[7]

It is here in this middle section that Goodman forges a reputation as an early post "modern" writer, or a writer of that "postwar disenchantment with Enlightenment conceptions of science, technology, truth, knowledge, and power relations." I would even say that his motivation for this "disenchantment" developed out of his increasing awareness that America's ambiguous pursuit for a "better living environment," through its application of the Enlightenment notion of progress, has led the people of America, ironically, to forfeit their freedom. In such a prophetic announcement, he says:

> It is becoming common among social philosophers to treat the progress of science and technology as if it now goes on by itself. [...] Whatever men wish, the independent development of scientific technology will shape the future. In more drastic versions of the theory, technology has already changed man into a product of itself, or man has become one special function in the technical system.(38)

Hence, America's faith in "progress" to bring "happiness" has a bit of irony to it, and this irony echoes the words of one of Kurt Vonnegut's characters in the novel, *Cat's Cradle*: "Americans ... are forever searching for love in forms it never takes, in places it can never be. It must have something to do with the vanished frontier"[8]

According to Goodman, this ironic pursuit of collective America is not an authentic pursuit of happiness, instead, Americans are attempting to rid themselves of an existential insecurity, and this insecurity is similar in form to the one mentioned earlier about those students "en masse":

> And the increasing moral and ritual drives to standardization, rationalization, control, and self-control—what Max Weber called the Protestant Ethic—have not, in my opinion, been mainly due to

---

[7] If Goodman were alive today, I wonder what he would have to say about online purchases, essentially allowing corporations to take money out of small communities without having any commitment to those communities.

[8] Claire Minton in *Cat's Cradle*, Dell Edition, 1998, p. 97.

technical routine but to new psychological obsessions to ward off insecurity, and compulsions to identify with power.(40)

"Collective America" has existential problems as well: obsessions to ward off "insecurity," "compulsions to identity" and inherent problems with "power." In fact, the collective is just a larger representation of those "mass" of students, or "Beat-aristocrats" mentioned earlier. But, both groups do approach a resolution oppositely. One by authenticating itself through a materialistic pursuit, while the other, younger, is the "anti-thesis" of it: theirs is a voluntary poverty. Hence, in the collective's pursuit to fulfill its "need" through materialism (i.e. consumerism) we come to realize that the means of the reactionary "mass student" movement of voluntary poverty was in fact on the same materialistic basis, yet a denial of it: voluntary poverty of their elder's insatiable consumerism, and this post-war consumerism, in Goodman's view, can't be separated from the notion of technology.

Goodman highlights the consequence of this "progressive" relationship between materialism and technology, and his government encourages

> [...] how to maximize technological growth to increase the abstract number of goods and services, whatever their quality or mutual *contradictions*. The check of the market has been weakened by subsidies, cost-plus contracts, monopolies, price-fixing, advertising, and the ignorance of consumers.(49; italics added)

Hence, Goodman enlightens us about an absurd idea that many Americans believe, which is that an immaterial or existential need, i.e. these "psychological obsessions," can be met through a materialistic pursuit, whether it is working toward a goal of "progress" in the economy for collective America, or towards an accumulation of consumer goods for each individual. According to Goodman Americans are searching for happiness "in forms it never takes, in places it can never be."

America's fetish with materialism is what Paul Goodman alludes to when he states that there is an inherent "metaphysical defect" in American democracy (94). The results of this defect are the moral ambiguities he follows throughout the book, and they have finally run their course on the lives of individuals in America today and in American politics. In addition, from what I understand about Goodman's descriptions of these ambiguities, they are similar (if not equal to) the "national inconsistencies" mentioned earlier in American history by Frederic Douglass, the emancipated slave, then black scholar. According to Douglass, these inconsistencies are the malicious "fruits" of America's failed experiment, and reading Douglass side by side with Goodman, it would appear that this "experiment" was doomed from its very beginning. Douglass says:

> You boast of your love of liberty, your superior civilization, and your pure Christianity, while the whole political power of the nation (as embodied in the two great political parties), is solemnly pledged to support and perpetuate the enslavement of three millions of your countrymen. [...] You can bare your bosom to the storm of British artillery to throw off a three penny tax on tea; and yet wring the last hard-earned farthing from the grasp of the black laborers of your country [....] You declare, before the world, and are understood by the world to declare, that you "hold these truths to be self evident, that all men are created equal; and are endowed by their Creator with certain inalienable rights; and that, among these are, life, liberty, and the pursuit of happiness;" and yet, you hold securely, in a bondage which, according to your own Thomas Jefferson, "is worse than ages of that which your fathers rose in rebellion to oppose," a seventh part of the [black] inhabitants of your country.[9]

These "inconsistencies" appear to be manifestations of a 'defective" model, but surely not the Enlightenment model where "truths" are supposed to be "self evident" (i.e. that all men are created equal) and are written into the "letter" of various laws. But if these truths are so self-evident, how do these ambiguities (or inconsistencies) come about, then? Perhaps these Enlightenment "ideals" were not followed seriously, or at least allowed to be exercised freely? This appears to be the case throughout American history. For instances,

---

[9] "Meeting sponsored by the Rochester Ladies' Anti-Slavery Society, Rochester Hall, Rochester, N.Y." The speech was originally published as a pamphlet. It can be located in James M. Gregory's, *Frederick Douglass: The Orator* (New York, 1893), 103-06.

individuals like Thomas Jefferson could formulate certain "rights" for each individual into that Enlightenment model of the American Constitution, and believe earnestly "that all men are created equal; and are endowed by their Creator with certain inalienable rights" yet profit from owning slaves himself.

According to Douglass, Goodman, and Reinhold Niebuhr, this failed model may have "infected" America when Americans choose to formulate their own "national dream" based on either (or both) "the Calvinistic or Jeffersonian concept of...national destiny."[10] The Calvinistic one, as one might guess, was a moral vision of American society, and ethics, virtue, was based in the character of the Old Testament God. The other, Jeffersonian, was secular. This secular stream of "virtue" "ethics," and "morality" was borrowed from the humanist tradition of the Enlightenment.

> The hope was that the earth could be transformed from a place of misery to an abode of happiness and contentment. The [Enlightenment] philosophy which generated this hope was intent both upon eliminating the natural hazards to comfort, security and contentment; and upon reforming society so that the privileges of life would be shared equitably.[11]

This "pursuit of happiness" which ought to "be shared equitably" explains why Goodman in *The Moral Ambiguity of America* spends much of his energy holding America to its preferred Enlightenment ideals. Therefore, to read Goodman is to understand the consequences of America's ambiguous embrace of the Enlightenment ideals. Also, if the Enlightenment was about equality for all human beings, and the American constitution entrenched this ideal in its frame work, then Goodman's pursuit (and passion) has been to make America live up to it, or else like an Old Testament prophet, he will play the role of the iconoclast and smash all its "defects" to pieces.

This is why I believe in the final chapters of *The Moral Ambiguity of America* (or its final section), he offers several insightful solutions

---

[10] Reinhold Niebuhr, *The Irony of American History*, ed. Andrew J. Bacevich (2008), 70.
[11] Ibid., 43.

to correcting these "metaphysical defects," yet holding on to the Enlightenment model which was pursued just as passionately by those founding members:

> Everybody knows that America is great because America is free; and by freedom is not finally meant the juridical freedom of the European tradition, freedom under law, having the legal rights and duties of citizens; what is meant is the spontaneous freedom of anarchy, opportunity to do what you can, although hampered by necessary conventions, as few as possible.(104)

Goodman's notion of freedom echoes the words of Emmanuel Kant: "For enlightenment of this kind, all that is needed is *freedom.*"[12] For the American experiment to function properly, it must, like of old, Goodman says, be "populist," or decentralized, pluralist, and based on the Enlightenment idea of "authentic" freedom. A Freedom that is not "juridical freedom", nor "freedom under the law", but the "spontaneous freedom of anarchy" like that of the revolutionaries of the American past (99). Simply put, freedom from tyranny. Hence, this is why *The Moral Ambiguity of America* presents numerous case examples of students and black Americans fighting for their freedom against tyrannical government bureaucracies, corporate America and its reliance on technology without much of a moral concern for the implications, and finally, how these unresolved concerns (that remain even today) have led them, and especially Goodman, to believe that without a "decentralized" response, democracy is not viable.

---

[12] Emmanuel Kant, "An Answer to the Question: 'What is Enlightenment?'"

I want to thank Susan Goodman, the Goodman family, and Taylor Stoehr for graciously helping to achieve this project.

THE EMPTY SOCIETY

During Eisenhower's second administration, I wrote a book describing how hard it was for young people to grow up in the corporate institutions of American society. Yet statistics at that time indicated that most were content to be secure as personnel of big corporations; a few deviated in impractical, and certainly unpolitical, ways, like being Beat[13] or delinquent. The system itself, like its President, operated with a cheerful and righteous self-satisfaction. There were no signs of its being vulnerable, though a loud chorus of intellectual critics, like myself, were sounding off against it. We were spoil-sports.

Less than ten years later, the feeling is different; it turns out that we critics were not altogether unrealistic. The system of institutions is still grander and more computerized, but it seems to have lost its morale. The baronial corporations are making immense amounts of money and are more openly and heavily subsidized by the monarch in Washington. The processing of the young is extended for longer years and its tempo speeded up. More capital and management are exported, interlocking with international capital, and more of the world (including Canada) is brought under American control. When necessary, remarkable military technology is brought to bear. At home, there is no political check, for no matter what the currents of

---

[13] The Beat Generation refers to a group of American post-WWII writers who came to prominence in the 1950s, as well as the cultural phenomena that they both documented and inspired. Central elements of "Beat" culture included experimentation with drugs, alternative forms of sexuality, an interest in Eastern religion, and a rejection of materialism by their "voluntary poverty."

opinion, by and large the dominant system wreaks its will, managing the parliamentary machinery to look like consensus.

Nevertheless, the feeling of justification is gone. Sometimes we seem to be bulling it through only in order to save face. Often, enterprises seem to be expanding simply because the managers cannot think of any other use of energy and resources. The economy is turning into a war economy. There are warnings of ecological disaster, pollution, congestion, poisoning, mental disease, anomie.[14] We have discovered that there is hardcore poverty at home that not easy to liquidate. Unlike the success of the Marshall Plan[15] in Europe in the Forties, it increasingly appears that poverty and unrest in Asia, Africa, and South America are not helped by our methods of assistance, but are perhaps made worse. There are flashes of suspicion, like flashes of lightning, that the entire system may be unviable. Influential senators refer to our foreign policy as "arrogant" and "lawless" but, in my opinion, our foreign and domestic system is all of a piece and is more innocent and deadly than that; it is mindless and morally insensitive. Its pretended purposes are window-dressing for purposeless expansion and a panicky need to keep things under control.

And now very many young people no longer want to cooperate with such a system. Indeed, a large and rapidly growing number—already more than 5% of college students—use language that is openly revolutionary and apocalyptic, as if in their generation they were going to make a French Revolution. More and more often, direct civil disobedience seems to make obvious sense.

We are exerting more power and feeling less right—what does that mean for the future? I have heard serious people argue for three plausible yet drastically incompatible predictions about America during the next generation, none of them happy:

---

[14] Goodman uses this term often so I will take the liberty to define it for the reader. Goodman means "general lawlessness" or "lack of social or moral standards in an individual or society." Also, it should not be interpreted as "anarchy."

[15] The Marshall Plan was the large-scale American program to aid Europe where the United States gave monetary support to help rebuild European economies after the end of World War II in order to combat the spread of Soviet communism. The plan was in operation for four years beginning in April 1948.

(1) Some feel, with a kind of Virgilian despair, that the American empire will succeed and will impose for a long time, at home and abroad, its meaningless management and showy style of life. For instance, we will "win" in Vietnam, though such a victory of brute military technology will be a moral disaster. Clubbing together with the other nuclear powers, we will stave off the nuclear war and stop history with a new Congress of Vienna. American democracy will vanish into an establishment of promoters, mandarins, and technicians, though for a while maintaining an image of democracy as in the days of Augustus and Tiberius.[16] And all this is probably the best possible outcome, given the complexities of high technology, urbanization, mass education, and over-population.

(2) Others believe, with dismay and horror, that our country is over-reaching and is bound for doom; but nothing can be done because policy cannot be influenced. Controlling communications, creating incidents that it then mistakes for history, deceived by its own Intelligence agents, our system is mesmerized. Like the Mikado, Washington is captive of its military-industrial complex. The way we manage the economy and technology must increase anomie and crime. Since the war-economy eats up brains and capital, we will soon be a fifth-rate economic power.[17] With a few setbacks abroad—for instance, when we force a major South American country to become communist—and with the increasing disorder on the streets that is inevitable because our cities are unworkable, there will be a police state. The atom bombs may then go off. Such being the forecast, the part of wisdom is escape, and those who cultivate LSD are on the right track.

(3) Others hold that the Americans are too decent to succumb to fascism, and too spirited to remain impotent clients of a man-

---

[16] Two of the first five Roman Emperors: Augustus, Tiberius, Caligula (also known as Gaius), Claudius, and Nero.

[17] In the July 25, 2011, Address to the Nation, U.S. President Barak Obama's dealt with the issue of government default, and the possibility of not paying the wages of thirty-five million public employees. Also, President Obama mentioned that the two wars in the middle-east (with Iraq and Afghanistan) and an overburdening health care system were the causes for the July 25 crisis.

agerial elite, and the tide of protest will continue to rise. The excluded poor are already refusing to remain excluded and they cannot be included without salutary changes. With the worst will in the world we cannot police the world. But the reality is that we are confused. We do not know how to cope with the new technology, the economy of surplus, the fact of One World that makes national boundaries obsolete, the unworkability of traditional democracy. We must invent new forms. To be sure, the present climate of emergency is bad for the social invention and experiment that are indispensable, and there is no doubt that our over-centralized and Establishment methods of organization make everybody stupid from top to bottom. But there is hope precisely in the young. They understand the problem in their bones. Of course, they don't know much and their disaffection both from tradition and from the adult world makes it hard for them to learn anything. Nevertheless, we will learn in the inevitable conflict, which will hopefully be mainly non-violent.

I myself hold this third view: American society is on a bad course, but there is hope for reconstruction through conflict. It is a wish. The evidence, so far, is stronger for either our empty success or for crack-up. My feeling is the same as about the atom bombs. Rationally, I must judge that the bombs are almost certain to go off in this generation; yet I cannot believe that they will go off, for I do not lead my life with that expectation.

Let me stop a moment and make another comparison. Thirty years ago the Jews in Germany believed that Hitler did not mean to exterminate them; "nobody," they said, "can be that stupid." So they drifted to the gas chambers, and went finally even without resistance. Now the nuclear powers continue stockpiling bombs and pouring new billions into missiles, antimissile missiles, and armed platforms in orbit. You Canadians, like us Americans, do not prevent it. Afterwards, survivors, if there are any, will ask, "How did we let it happen?"

I am eager, as well as honored, to be talking to a Canadian audience on the state of American society, and especially to the Canadian young. You people are not yet so wrongly committed as we. Your land is less despoiled, your cities are more manageable, you are not yet so sold on mass mis-education. You are not in the trap of militarism.[18] A large minority of you are deeply skeptical of American methods and oppose the unquestioned extension of American power. Some of us Americans have always wistfully hoped that you Canadians would teach us a lesson or two, though, to be frank, you have usually let us down.

2

In these lectures on our ambiguous position, I shall have to talk a good deal about style. To illustrate the current style of American enterprise, let me analyze a small, actual incident. It is perfectly typical, banal; no one would raise his eyebrows at it, it is business as usual.

Washington has allotted several billions of dollars to the schools. The schools are not teaching very well, but there is no chance that anybody will upset the apple-cart and ask if so much doing of lessons is the right way to educate the young altogether. Rather, there is a demand for new "methods" and mechanical equipment, which will disturb nobody, and electronics is the latest thing that every forward-looking local school board must be proud to buy. So to cut in on this melon, electronics corporations, IBM, Xerox, etc., have hastened to combine with, or take over, textbook houses. My own publisher, Random House, has been bought up by the Radio Corporation of America.

Just now, General Electric and Time, Inc., that owns a textbook house, have put nearly 40 millions into a joint subsidiary called General Learning. And an editor of Life magazine has been relieved of his duties for five weeks, in order to prepare a prospectus on the broad educational needs of America and the world, to come up with exciting proposals, so that General Learning can move with purpose

---

[18] Military spending has reached $22.3 billion (in 2010-2011), according to a report by the Canadian Centre for Policy Alternatives authored by Rideau Institute senior advisor Bill Robinson–54% higher than before the terrorist attacks of September 11, 2001.

into this unaccustomed field. The editor has collected and is boning up on the latest High Thought on education, and in due course he invites me to lunch, to pick my brains for something new and radical. "The sky," he assures me, "is the limit." (I am known, let me explain, as a severe critic of the school establishment.) "Perhaps," he tells me at lunch, "there is no unique place for General Learning. They'll probably end up as prosaic makers of school hardware. But we ought to give it a try."

Consider the premises of this odd situation, where first they have the organization and the technology, and then they try to dream up a use for it. In the 18th century, Adam Smith[19] thought that one started with the need and only then collected capital to satisfy it. In the 19th century there was already a lot of capital to invest, but by and large the market served as a check, to guarantee utility, competence, and relevance. Now, however, the subsidy removes the check of the market and a promotion can expand like weeds in a well-manured field. The competence required is to have a big organization and sales force, and to be in, to have the prestige and connections plausibly to get the subsidy. Usually it is good to have some minimal relation to the ostensible function, e.g. a textbook subsidiary related to schooling or Time-Life related to, let us say, learning. But indeed, when an expanding corporation becomes very grand, it generates an expertise of its own called Systems Development, applicable to anything. For example, as an expert in Systems Development, North American Aviation is hired to reform the penal system of California; there is no longer need to demonstrate acquaintance with any particular human function.

Naturally, with the divorce of enterprise from utility and competence, there goes a heavy emphasis on rhetoric and public relations to prove utility and competence. So an editor must be re-assigned for five weeks to write a rationale. It is his task to add ideas or talking points to the enterprise, like a wrapper. The personnel of expanding corporations, of course, are busy people and have not had time to think of many concrete ideas; they can, however, phone writers and concerned professionals. Way-out radicals, especially, do

---

[19] Scottish economist (1723-1790) and known for, *The Wealth of Nations*.

a lot of thinking, since they have little practical employment. And since the enterprise is free-floating anyway, it is dandy to include, in the prospectus, something daring, or even meaningful. (Incidentally, I received no fee, except the lunch and pleasant company; but I did pick up an illustration for these lectures.)

In an affluent society that can afford it, there is something jolly about such an adventure of the electronics giant, the mighty publisher, the National Science Foundation that has made curriculum studies, and local school boards that want to be in the swim. Somewhere down the line, however, this cabal of decision-makers is going to coerce the time of life of real children and control' the activity of classroom teachers. These, who are directly engaged in the human function of learning and teaching, have no say in what goes on. This introduces a more sober note. Some of the product of the burst of corporate activity and technological virtuosity will be useful, some not—the pedagogical evidence is mixed and not extensive—but the brute fact is that the children are quite incidental to the massive intervention of the giant combinations.

I have chosen a wry example. But I could have chosen the leader of the American economy, the complex of cars, oil, and roads. This outgrew its proper size perhaps thirty years ago; now it is destroying both the cities and the countryside, and has been shown to be careless of even elementary safety.

Rather, let me turn abruptly to the Vietnam War. We notice the same family traits. Whatever made us embark on this adventure, by now we can define the Vietnam War as a commitment looking for a reason, or at least a rationalization. There has been no lack of policy-statements, rhetorical gestures, (it seems) manufactured incidents, and (certainly) plain lies; but as the war has dragged on and grown, all these have proved to be mere talking-points. Ringing true, however, has been the fanfare about the superb military technology that we have deployed. The theme is used as a chief morale-builder for the troops. In the absence of adequate political reasons, some have even said that the war is largely an occasion for testing new hardware and techniques. It is eerie to hear, on the TV, an airman enthusiastically praise the split-second scheduling of his missions to devastate rice-fields. Such appreciation of know-how is a cheerful American disposition, but it does not do much credit to him as a grown man.

Yet what emerges most strikingly from our thinking about and prosecution of the Vietnam War is, again, the input-output accounting, the systems development, and the purely incidental significance of the human beings involved. The communiques are concerned mainly with the body-count of V.C. in ratio to our own losses, since there is a theory that in wars of this kind one must attain a ratio of 5 to 1 or 10 to 1. According to various estimates, it costs $50,000 to $250,000 to kill 1 Vietnamese, hopefully an enemy. Similarly, the bombing of civilians and the destruction of their livelihood occur as if no human beings were involved; they are officially spoken of as unfortunate but incidental. (The average indemnity for a civilian death is $34.) We claim that we have no imperialist aims in Vietnam—though we are building air-bases of some very heavy concrete and steel—but evidently old-fashioned imperialism was preferable, since it tried to keep the subjugated population in existence, for taxes and labor.[20]

At home, correspondingly, college students are deferred from the draft because they will be necessary to man the professions and scientific technology, while farm boys, black Americans, and Spanish Americans are drafted because they are otherwise good for nothing. That is to say, war is not regarded as a dread emergency, in which each one does his bit, but as part of the on-going business of society, in which fighting and dying are usual categories of the division of labor. But this is bound to be the case when 20% of the Gross National Product is spent on war[21] (using a multiplier of 2); when more than half of the gross new investment since 1945 has been in war industry; and when much of higher education and science is devoted to war technology.

---

[20] For an excellent understanding of the Vietnam/US conflict, see Stanley Karnow's *Vietnam: A History*. New York: Penguin Books, 1991.
[21] These figures today range from 36% to 54% of the GDP depending how the U.S. budget is interpreted.

The Americans are not a warlike or bloodthirsty people, though violent. The dehumanizing of war is part of a general style of enterprise and control in which human utility and even the existence of particular human beings are simply not a paramount consideration. Great armaments manufacturers have said that they are willing and ready to convert their capital and skill to peaceful production when given the signal; this seems to mean that it is indifferent to them what they enterprise. Studies of American workers[22] have shown that they take their moral and esthetic standards not from family, church, friends, or personal interests, but from the organization and style of work at the plant; and I think that this explains the present peculiar situation that other nations of the world regard our behavior in the Vietnam War with a kind of horror, whereas Americans sincerely talk as if it were a messy job to be done as efficiently as possible.

This brings us to a broader question: What do we mean by technical efficiency in our system?

3

Corporate and bureaucratic societies, whether ruled by priests, mandarins, generals, or business managers, have always tended to diminish the importance of personal needs and human feeling, in the interest of abstractions and systemic necessities. And where there has been no check by strong community ties, effective democracy, or a free market, it has not been rare for the business of society to be largely without utility or common sense. Nevertheless, modern corporate societies that can wield a high technology are liable to an unique temptation: since they do not exploit common labor, they may tend to exclude the majority of human beings altogether, as useless for the needs of the system and therefore as not quite persons.

---

[22] "workmen" in the original document. All other usages of "workmen" have been changed to "workers".

This has been the steady tendency in America. The aged are ruled out at an earlier age, the young until a later age. We have liquidated most small farmers. There is no place for the poor, e.g., more than 20 million black Americans[23] and Latin Americans. A rapidly increasing number are certified as insane or otherwise incompetent. These groups already comprise more than a majority of the population. Some authorities say (though others deny) that with full automation most of the rest will also be useless.

There is nothing malevolent or heartless in the exclusion. The tone is not like that of the old exploitative society when people were thrown out of work during the lows of the business cycle. For humane and political reasons, even extraordinary efforts are made to shape the excluded into the dominant style, so they can belong. Even though the system is going to need only a few percent with elaborate academic training, all the young are subjected to twelve years of schooling and 40% go to college. There is every kind of training and social service to upgrade the poor and to make the handicapped productive members of society. At high cost of effort and suffering, mentally retarded children must be taught to read, if only "cat" and "rat."

But a frank look shows, I think, that, for most, the long schooling is a way of keeping the young on ice; the job training is busy-work; and the social services turn people into "community dependents" for generations. Much of the anxiety about the "handicapped" and the "underprivileged" is suburban squeamishness that cannot tolerate difference. What is never done, however, is to change the rules of the system, to re-define usefulness in terms of how people are, and to shape the dominant style to people. This cannot be done because it would be inefficient and, indeed, degrading, for there is only one right way to exist. Do it our way or else you are not quite a person.

---

[23] Paul Goodman originally used the term "Negroes" here, and the publisher has taken the liberty to replace it throughout the entire book. However, we must not think that Paul Goodman is using this term in a derogatory sense because many "Negros" during the 1960s, including Dr. Martin Luther King Jr., referred to themselves as this. Also, the current figures today for both are, 38.9 million African Americans and 28 million Latin Americans.

Inevitably, such self-righteous inflexibility is self-mesmerizing and self-proving, for other methods and values are not allowed to breathe and prove themselves. Often it would be cheaper to help people to be in their own way or at least to let them be; but anything in a different or outmoded style has "deviant" or "underprivileged" written on it, and no expense is spared to root it out, in the name of efficiency. Thus, it would have been cheaper to pay the small farmers to stay put if they wished. (Anyway, I shall try to show in a subsequent lecture[24], it is not the case in many situations that small farming and local distribution are less efficient than the plantations and national chain-grocers that have supplanted them with the connivance of government policy.) It would be far cheaper to give money directly to the urban poor to design their own lives, rather than to try to make them shape up; it has been estimated that, in one area of poverty in New York City, the cost per family in special services is more than $10,000 a year;[25] and anyway, to a candid observer, the culture of poverty is not inferior to that of the middle class, if it were allowed to be decent, if it could be, in Péguy's distinction, pauvreté rather than misère. Very many of the young would get a better education and grow up usefully to themselves and society if the school-money were used for real apprenticeships, or even if they were given the school-money to follow their own interests, ambitions, and even fancies, rather than penning them for lengthening years in increasingly regimented institutions; anyway, many young people could enter many professions without most of the schooling if we changed the rules for licensing and hiring. But none of these simpler and cheaper ways would be "efficient"; the clinching proof is that they would be hard to administer.

Also, are the people useless? The concept of efficiency is largely, maybe mainly, systemic. It depends on the goals of the

---

[24] Paul Goodman will take this topic up in chapter four.

[25] As of July 1988 (20 years later), this amount did not change. A family of four, in New York City, received a maximum of $837 a month. Also, there were 1.3. million receiving benefits (*New York Times*, July 24, 1988). In 2007, this number increased to 3 million and involved a 5 billion dollar budget (Wikipedia: The New York City Human Resources Administration/Department of Social Services).

system, which may be too narrowly and inflexibly conceived; it depends on the ease of administration, which is considered as more important than economic or social costs; but it depends also on the method of calculating costs, which may create a false image of efficiency by ruling out "intangibles" that do not suit the method. This source of error becomes very important in advanced urban economies where the provision of personal and social services grows rapidly in proportion to hardware and food production and distribution. In providing services, whether giving information, selling, teaching children, admitting to college, assigning jobs, serving food, or advising on welfare, standardization and punch-cards may seem to fulfill the functions, but they may do so at the expense of frayed nerves, waiting in line, bad mistakes, misfitting, and cold soup. In modern conditions, the tailor-made improvisations of fallible but responsive human beings may be increasingly indispensable rather than useless. In the jargon of Frank Riessman, there is a need for "sub-professionals." Yet the mass-production and business-machine style, well adapted to manufacturing hardware and calculating logistics, will decide that people are useless anyway, since they can theoretically be dispensed with. It is a curious experience to hear a gentleman from the Bureau of the Budget explain the budget of the War on Poverty according to cost-benefit computation. He can demonstrate that the participation of the poor in administering a program is disadvantageous; he can show you the flow chart; he cannot understand why poor people make a fuss on this point. It is useless to explain to him that they do not trust the program (nor the director) but would like to get the money for their own purposes.

Abroad, the Americans still engage in plenty of old-fashioned exploitation of human labor, as in Latin America; yet the tendency is again to regard the underdeveloped peoples as not quite persons, and to try to shape them up by (sometimes) generous assistance in our own style. For example, one of the radical ideas of General Learning, the subsidiary of General Electric and Time, Inc., is to concentrate on electronic devices to teach literacy to the masses of children in poor countries; we must export our Great Society. Our enterprisers are eager to build highways and pipelines through the jungle, to multiply bases for our airplanes, and to provide other items of the

American standard of living, for which the western-trained native political leaders have "rising aspirations." Unfortunately, this largesse must often result in disrupting age-old cultures, fomenting tribal wars, inflating prices and wages and reducing decent poverty to starvation, causing the abandonment of farms and disastrous instant urbanization, making dictatorships inevitable, and drawing simple peoples into Great Power conflicts. And woe if they do not then shape up, if they want to develop according to their local prejudices, for instance for land reform. They become an uncontrollable nuisance, surely therefore allied with our enemies, and better dead than Red.[26] In his great speech in Montreal, Secretary McNamara[27] informed us that since 1958, 87% of the very poor nations and 69% of the poor nations, but only 48% of the middle income nations, have had serious violent disturbances. The cure for it, he said, was development, according to the criteria of our cash economy, while protected from subversion by our bombers. How to explain to this arithmetically astute man that he is not taking these people seriously as existing?

A startlingly literal corollary of the principle that our system excludes human beings rather than exploits them is the agreement of all liberals and conservatives that there must be a check on population growth, more especially among backward peoples and the poor at home. We are definitely beyond the need for the labor of the "proletariat" ("producers of offspring") and the Iron Law of Wages to keep that labor cheap. Yet I am bemused by this unanimous recourse to a biological and mathematical etiology for our troubles. Probably there is a danger of world-overpopulation in the foreseeable future. (The United States, though, is supposed to level off at 300 millions in 2020 [28], and this would not be a dense

---

[26] Communist.

[27] Robert McNamara was an American business executive and the eighth Secretary of Defense, serving under Presidents John F. Kennedy and Lyndon B. Johnson from 1961 to 1968, during which time he played a large role in escalating the United States involvement (up to 500, 000 soldiers) in the Vietnam War.

[28] As of December 2011, the U.S. population is 312,850,000.

population for our area.) Certainly with the likelihood of nuclear war there is a danger of world-underpopulation. However, until we institute more human ecological, economic, and political arrangements, I doubt that population control is the first order of business; nor would I trust the Americans to set the rules.

4

In this lecture, I have singled out two trends of the dominant organization of American society, its increasing tendency to expand, meaninglessly, for its own sake, and its tendency to exclude human beings as useless. It is the Empty Society, the obverse face of the Affluent Society. When Adam Smith spoke of the Wealth of Nations, he did not mean anything like this.

The meaningless expansion and the excluding are different things, but in our society they are essentially related. Lack of meaning begins to occur when the immensely productive economy over-matures and lives by creating demand instead of meeting it; when the check of the free market gives way to monopolies, subsidies, and captive consumers; when the sense of community vanishes and public goods are neglected and resources despoiled; when there is made-work (or war) to reduce unemployment; and when the measure of economic health is not increasing well-being but abstractions like the Gross National Product and the rate of growth.

Human beings tend to be excluded when a logistic style becomes universally pervasive, so that values and data that cannot be standardized and programmed are disregarded; when function is adjusted to the technology rather than technology to function; when technology is confused with autonomous science, a good in itself, rather than being limited by political and moral prudence; when there develops an establishment of managers and experts who alone license and allot resources, and it deludes itself that it knows the only right method and is omnicompetent. Then common people become docile clients, maintained by sufferance, or they are treated as deviant.

It is evident that, for us, these properties of the empty society are essentially related. If we did not exclude so many as not really persons, we would have to spend more of our substance on worthwhile goods, including subsistence goods, both at home and abroad; we would have to provide a more human environment for the children to grow up in; there would be more paths to grow up and more ways of being a person. On the other hand, if we seriously and efficiently tackled the problems of anomie, alienation, riot, pollution, congestion, urban blight, degenerative and mental disease, etc., we would find ourselves paying more particular attention to persons and neighborhoods, rather than treating them as standard items; we would have a quite different engineering and social science; and we would need all the human resources available.

Certainly we would stop talking presumptuously about The Great Society[29] and find ourselves struggling, in the confusing conditions of modern times, for a decent society.

The chief danger to American society at present, and to the world from American society, is our mindlessness, induced by empty institutions. It is a kind of mesmerism, a self-delusion of formal Tightness, that affects both leaders and people. We have all the talking-points but less and less content. The Americans are decent people, generous and fairly compassionate. They are not demented and fanatical, like some other imperial powers of the past and present, but on the contrary rather skeptical and with a sense of humor. They are not properly called arrogant, though perhaps presumptuous. But we have lost our common sense, for which we were once noted. This kind of intelligence was grounded not in history or learning, nor in finesse of sensibility and analysis, but in the habit of making independent judgments and in democratically rubbing shoulders with all kinds and conditions. We have lost it by becoming personnel of a mechanical system and exclusive suburbanites, by getting out of contact with real jobs and real people. We suddenly have developed an Establishment, but our leaders do

---

[29] A slogan of President Lyndon B. Johnson in 1964 advocating greater educational and job-training opportunities for American youth, redevelopment of housing in the cities, better medical care for the aged, and measures for the alleviation of poverty. This program was undermined by Johnson's efforts in the Vietnam War.

not have the tradition and self-restraint to come on like an establishment. Thus, we are likely to wreak havoc not because of greed, ideology, or arrogance, but because of a bright strategy of the theory of games and an impatient conviction that other people don't know what's good for them.

COUNTER-FORCES FOR A DECENT SOCIETY   II

In the first lecture, I depicted my country as bound on a course that must lead either to an empty and immoral empire or to exhaustion and fascism. There is evidence for both gloomy pictures. Let me now mention some counter-forces and give evidence for a future of more decency. These forces seem weaker and, except for court decisions, they do not constitute official policy nor control technology. Yet they are wonderfully stubborn and show flashes of power. And of course the traditional American sentiment is that a decent society cannot be built by dominant official policy but only by grass-roots resistance, community development, social invention, and citizenly vigilance to protect liberty. These, surprisingly, are reviving. In any case, if, even with good intentions, the interlocking corporate style destroys vitality, an increasing ragged conflict (hopefully without much violence) might at present be our best hope.

The ambiguity of values in America is really striking. Often it is as if there were a line down the front page of *The New York Times,* with half of the stories making one despondent, afraid, or indignant and half cheerful, hopeful, and proud. Needless to say, the trends that please me are called un-American[30] by some; but you will recognize them as classically American. *The question is whether or not our*

---

[30] Paul Goodman seems to be alluding to the House Committee on Un-American Activities (HCUA), which was an investigative committee of the United States House of Representatives. Under this mandate, the committee focused its investigations on real and suspected communists in positions of actual or supposed influence in the United States society.

beautiful libertarian, pluralist, and populist [31] experiment is viable in modern conditions. If it's not, I don't know any other acceptable politics, and I'm a man without a country.

With a few exceptions, the Supreme Court has been extending liberty of publication, art, assembly, and political action. It has condoned flagrant examples of civil disobedience. Even more significant are its decisions limiting the police, forbidding wiretapping and forced confession, and tightening due process, for here the conflict with the system is evident. The trend of the government, the suburbs, etc., is toward more police, equipped with a powerful technology, and instant national and international connections; but the Court and a stubborn group of lawyers and sociologists seem determined to resist unchecked police power and draconian punishments. Capital punishment is being rather rapidly abolished, largely, I think, because of the general revulsion, well expressed by Camus,[32] against the mechanical State snuffing out a life. New York and the District of Columbia have reformed the bail system, to rescue the poor from rotting in jail before trial, and other states will follow suit. These reforms are the reverse of the moral insensitivity I spoke of in my first lecture. It is not 1984.[33] We are as yet unwilling to identify with the system in which we nevertheless act.

Some cities have adopted civilian boards to review complaints against the police. (But New York has just voted its board out of existence: these cases are touch and go.) Legislation is proposed for a Public Defender to offset the advantage of the State Attorney's staff and business machines. There is talk of an ombudsman to review complaints against government bureaucracy. Almost invariably, to be sure, such agencies, like the regulatory agencies in Washington, end up in coalition with what they are supposed to regulate; they cushion

---

[31] Goodman elaborates on these terms in Chapter Six.

[32] The French existentialist writer, Albert Camus. See for example, *The Rebel* (1956).

[33] George Orwell's *1984.*

protest rather than remedy abuses; nevertheless, they do indicate an awakening alarm about total control. Unwilling to alter the framework, people hanker for a kind of Roman tribune to intervene with his drastic personal vote. A better proposal, in my opinion, is for disadvantaged groups, like Black Americans, to police their own neighborhoods according to their own mores.

Puritanism persists, yet there is a remarkable shift away from moralism and hypocrisy, and toward plain inconsistency. For instance, narcotics laws are strengthened and extended to LSD and other non-addictives; but there is a strong campaign for the English system for the addictive drugs, and champions of LSD have a messianic fervor, claiming that the issue is between conformism and a personal or religious way of life. We have the odd situation that penalties become heavier while public opinion is more and more uncertain.

The continuing sexual revolution deserves special notice. Here the inconsistency between High Thought and the repressive laws and sexless schools is blatant. But the most practical change has been not the actual sexual behavior of the adolescents and adults, which so far has not produced much poetry or deep joy, though it is better than the sexual climate in which I grew up; rather, it is the now widely accepted freedom of the children, the relaxed toilet-training, permitted masturbation, nakedness, informal dress. A generation ago we were warned that this freedom would produce an unruly brood; it has, and I like the results. Correspondingly, counter to the gigantism and stepped up schedule, curriculum, and grading of the official schools, there is a revival of progressive schools, and inevitably these veer toward A. S. Neill's Summerhill,[34] freeing the children from compulsory attendance and giving them a say in the school

---

[34] Alexander Sutherland Neill (1883-1973) was founder of Summerhill school. Neill believed that the happiness of the child should be the paramount consideration in decisions about the child's upbringing, and that this happiness grew from a sense of personal freedom.

administration. Progressive education belongs, of course, to only a few middle class families; yet the Freedom Schools[35] of the black American revolution are pedagogically not so very different.

There is a revival in the churches. Long pillars of the establishment, they too have begun to take alarm that the establishment is becoming anti-human; and we find clergymen in the unlikely position of fighting for migrant farm-workers and against the drug and sex laws, and confessing that God is *not* on our side in Vietnam and in manufacturing nuclear bombs. The churches have latched onto non-directive community-development. Some of them have sponsored the most daring, and unofficious, protest organizations and legal defense for black Americans and Spanish-Americans. In New York City, the best community theaters—indeed the best theaters—are in churches; nor are the plays lacking in dirty words. And on many college campuses, the young existentialist chaplain—or even the Catholic—is the center of radical student activity.

There is an odd explosion in the arts, with an immense number of amateurs, of a kind of urban folk art in all genres. It is entirely inauthentic in style, combining misunderstood fragments of international culture with commercialized mountain music and stereotyped urban naturalism; yet it is authentic to the actual urban confusion. On a more intellectual level, there have been lovely sporadic attempts to enliven the cities with happenings in the park, spontaneous fence painting, and vest-pocket playgrounds laid out by adolescents. Unfortunately, since the urban folk have neither tradition nor resources and their art is largely an outcry of alienation, there is no popular effort to cope with the big horrors of urban ugliness and pollution; even so, what the people do has more vitality

---

[35] Schools that opened in protest to state laws against educating blacks. The earliest schools were founded by whites, Elias Neau (1704) in New York City and by Quakers, led by Anthony Benezet, in Philadelphia (1770).

than the synthetic culture-centers sponsored by government and foundations.

Economically, there is an increase in minimum wages and unionization of the most exploited groups, hospital attendants and migrant farmhands. More significantly, there is a growing sentiment, which I think will prevail, for a guaranteed minimum income, which would be far preferable, in the United States, to the present system of welfare payments and social services. It would be a giant step toward making decent poverty possible, reopening independent choice of how to live, and encouraging small businesses and rural reconstruction. It would loosen top-down control.

The most spectacular battle with American business-as-usual-and-more-so has been, of course, the belated movement for black emancipation. This has occurred, naturally, when the need to exploit field and unskilled labor has diminished and black Americans have joined the ranks of the simply excluded. Their refusal to be excluded has penetrated the moral obtuseness of some Americans, but the most far-reaching effect will be, in my opinion, the renewed political lesson, that people are taken seriously when they raise Cain[36] and insist on managing in their own way. Any help given by government—it has been small—has been because of local pressure, threat of riot, and riot. And, at least in the South, the movement has given remarkable proof that decentralized grass-roots action, loosely co-ordinated, can exert political power.

The black American movement is part of a tide of populist direct action rising throughout the nation. There are almost daily marches, boycotts, sit-ins, protest to the point of smashing chairs at City Council meetings, civil disobedience to the point of filling the

---

[36] When they raise hell. It is interesting that Goodman mentions this term here because he is discussing the implications of slavery and racism in the South, which of course go back as far as the American Civil War (a war between brothers also).

jails. This populism is called lawless, but, as I shall argue in a later lecture, it is the alternative to anomie and crime. Most of the actions are not constructive, there is rarely a political program; but they are necessary counter-actions to actions of the dominant system that are absurd, presumptuous, and finally intolerable. The protest against poisoning the milk with nuclear tests and boycott of the bomb-shelters were archetypal, and the mothers, high-school students, and famous scientists took to the streets, the principal's office, and the pages of *The New York Times*. So, neighborhoods rally en masse to stop high-handed Urban Renewal and Highway commissioners. Housewives picket super-markets because of inflationary prices. The League for Sexual Freedom parades with floats and dirty words. The hustlers and waifs of the Tenderloin in San Francisco organize for self-help and a voice in the local Economic Opportunity Council. Blacks march against a police outrage and end with a riot. Resentment at not being taken seriously by municipal social workers easily consolidates into organization a la Saul Alinsky.[37] Students sit down around an Administration spokesman on foreign policy because he will not answer their questions. Seven hundred students are arrested in Berkeley because the college administration has lied to them. It is a ferment of populism occurring, under urban conditions, because finally there is no other way to exist. Naturally, the Federal Bureau of Investigation has proved that it is all a Communist plot. The serious question, to which I shall return later, is a different one: will this urban populism succeed in reviving democracy, or will it be manipulated like the Roman mob in the time of Caesar?

With a populist sounding-board behind them, finally, muck-raking intellectuals always sound more for real. Atomic scientists,

---

[37] Saul David Alinsky was a Jewish American community organizer and writer. He is generally considered to be the founder of modern community organizing. In the 1930s, Alinsky organized the Back of the Yards Neighborhood campaign in Chicago (made infamous by Upton Sinclair's novel *The Jungle* for the horrific working conditions in the Union Stock Yards).

Rachel Carson, or Ralph Nader write books, and there is a flurry of Congressional investigation. Ingenuous college students imagine that the social criticism that they read in paperbacks is supposed to lead to action as well as being entertainment.

2

The most portentous libertarian and populist counter-force is the youth movement, and I shall devote to it the remainder of this lecture, for it expresses with remarkable precision, point by point, the opposition to the over-centralized, interlocking, and empty society.

About half the Americans are under 26. Nearly 40% of the college age group go to college. Of the present collegians–there are now 6 million[38] in 2,000 institutions–it is estimated that 5% are in some activity of the radical youth movement. This does not seem a great proportion, but it has increased at least tenfold in the last decade and it and the number of its alumni will certainly increase even more rapidly in the next years. More important, unlike the black Americans, the radical young are not only the middle-class collegians, graduate students, or graduates, but they are also disproportionately the best students and from the best schools. They are an economic force, looming large among the indispensable inheritors of the dominant power in society. And although–or perhaps because–they do not share a common ideology but rather a common sentiment and style, in showdown situations like the troubles in Berkeley[39] they

---

[38] According to the U.S. Census Bureau's Current Population Survey, there were 20.4 million students enrolled in 2009. Hence, 5 percent of 20.4 million would equal one million (National Centre for Educational Statistics).

[39] The Berkeley riots were a series of protests at and near the University of California, Berkeley in the 1960s. Many of these protests were a small part of the larger Free Speech Movement, which had national implications. These riots were headed under the informal

have shown a remarkable solidarity and a common detestation for the liberal Center, crossing even the apparent chasm between Extreme Right and Extreme Left.

A major reason for their solidarity and their increase is mass higher education itself. For most, this has little academic value, and one of the shared sentiments is resistance to being academically processed for the goals of the system; nevertheless, the colleges and universities are, in fact, many hundreds of physical and social communities of young people, with populations of a few thousand to 25,000, sharing a sub-culture, propagandizing one another, and learning to distrust anybody over 30. Such collections of youth are a social phenomenon unique in history. Consider some details from San Francisco State College, where I was hired by the Associated Students last spring. With 15,000 students, the Associated Students have $300,000 annually in student dues, more than half of which is free and clear and which they use for untraditional purposes including organizing a tenants' organization, helping delinquents in a reformatory, running a tutorial program for black Americans and Mexican children (with 300 collegian tutors), sponsoring a weekly television program, running an "experimental college" with twenty offbeat courses, and hiring their own professor. They apply on their own for grants from the Ford Foundation and the Poverty program!

Or consider the college press, with its fairly captive audience of several million, often daily. In a few cases, e.g. Harvard and Columbia, publication has gone off campus and is not under the tutelage of "faculty advisers." Increasingly, the college papers subscribe to news services and print (and edit) national and international news, and they also use syndicated material, like Art Buchwald, Feiffer, Russell Baker. Occasionally, notably the Cornell *Sun*, the college paper is the chief daily of its town. More important,

---

leadership of students Mario Savio, Brian Turner, Bettina Apthecker, Steve Weissman, Art Goldberg, Jackie Goldberg, and others.

there is a national student press service that could be a powerfully effective liaison for mobilizing opinion on common issues. Last winter I wrote a fortnightly column on student matters for a tiny college in Vermont, which the enterprising editor at once syndicated to fifty other college papers. On this model there could spring up a system of direct support, and control, of the students' "own" authors, just as, of course, they now indirectly support them through magazines whose main circulation is collegiate.

Nor are these young people properly called "youth." The exigencies of the American system have kept them in tutelage, doing lessons, till 23 and 24 years of age, years past when young industrial workers used to walk union picket-lines or when farmers carried angry pitchforks, or soldiers are now drafted into the army. Another cause of their shared resentment is the foolish attempt to arrest their maturation and regulate their social, sexual, and political activity.

Unlike the suburban practice of making acquaintance by role, status, or caste, these young live a good deal by "interpersonal relations" and are unusually careless, in their friendships, about status or getting ahead. I do not mean by this that they are especially affectionate or compassionate—they are averagely so—but they have been soaked in modern psychology, group therapy, sensitivity training; and as a style they go in for direct confrontation and sometimes brutal frankness. Add to this the lack of embarrassment due to animally uninhibited childhood. They are the post-Freudian generation—their parents were analyzed from 1920-1940! The effect—for example, long sessions of mutual analysis or jabber about LSD trips—can be tiresome, but it is pretty fatal to suburban squeamishness, race and moral prejudice, and maintaining appearances. And still another cause of resentment at the colleges is the impersonality and distance of the teachers and the big classes that make dialogue impossible.

Middle-class privacy vanishes. An innovation of the Beats was the community use of one another's pads, and this spirit of sharing has persisted in off-campus university communities, which are very different from paternalistic dormitories or fraternity row. In big cities there are growing bohemian student neighborhoods, tending to be located in racially mixed sections; and such neighborhoods, with their own coffee-houses and headquarters for student political clubs, cannot be controlled by campus administration. In the famous insurrection of Berkeley, Telegraph Avenue could easily rally 3,000 students, ex-students, wives, and pals. The response of the administration of the University of California has been, characteristically, to try to root up the neighborhood with Federally financed Urban Renewal!

The community meaning of the widespread use of hallucinogenic drugs is ambiguous. (Few students use addictives.) I have heard students hotly defend the drugs as a means of spiritual and political freedom, or hotly condemn them as a quietist opium of the people, or indifferently dismiss them as a matter of taste. But they do not operate like the chummy alcoholism of the fraternities, suburbs, and Washington; and, of course, being illegal and hard to procure, they tend to create conspiracy. The LSD cult[40] especially must be understood as part of a wave of religiosity that has included Zen, Christian and Jewish existentialism, a kind of psychoanalytic yoga, and the *Book of Changes*. We have seen that on the campus the young chaplain is often the center of action. Certainly the calculating rationalism of modern times is losing its self-evidence; and it is not the end of the world to go crazy temporarily.

---

[40] Goodman says later, in chapter five, that "Dr. Timothy Leary, the psychodelics man, espouses the extreme of this philosophy, 'Turn on, tune in, and drop out'; but I doubt that relying on chemicals is really a way of dropping out of our drug-ridden and technological society."

The shagginess and chosen poverty of the student communities have nuances that are immensely important. We must remember that these are the young of the affluent society, used to a high standard of living and confident that, if and when they want, they can fit in and make good money. Having suffered little pressure of insecurity, they have little psychological need to climb; just as, coming from impeccably respectable homes, they feel no disgrace about sitting a few nights in jail. By confidence they are aristocrats—en masse. At the same time, the affluent standard of living which they have seen is pretty synthetic and very much of it useless and phony, and the poverty of the students is not degraded or insecure but decent, natural, and in many ways more comfortable than their parents' standard, especially if they can always corral obvious goodies like hi-fi equipment and motorcycles. Typically, they tour Europe on nothing, sleeping under bridges; but if they get really hungry, they can drop in at American Express. Most of the major satisfactions of life, sex, paperback books, guitars, roaming, conversation, and activist politics, need cost little. Thus, they are the first generation in America selective of the standard of living; if this attitude became general, it would be a disaster for the expanding GNP. And there is an unmistakable tone of policy and defiance in their poverty and shagginess. They have been influenced by the Voluntary Poverty of the Beat movement, signifying withdrawal from the trap of the affluent economy. Finally, by acquaintance they experience the harsher tone of the involuntary poverty of the black Americans and Spanish Americans whose neighborhoods they visit and with whom they are friends.

3

The chief (conscious) drive of the radical young is their morality. As Mike Harrington has put it, "They drive you crazy with their morality," since for it they disregard prudence and politics, and they mercilessly condemn legitimate casuistry as if it were utterly phony. When politically minded student leaders, like–sometimes–the Students for a Democratic Society,[41] engage in "tactics" and the "art of the possible," they swiftly lose influence, whereas indignation or a point of honor will rally the young in droves.

Partly this drive to morality is the natural ingenuousness of youth, freed of the role-playing and status-seeking of our society. As aristocrats, not driven by material or ulterior motives, they will budge for ideals or not at all. Partly their absolutism is a disgusted reaction to cynicism and the prevalent adult conviction that "nothing can be done, you can't fight City Hall, modern life is too complex." But mostly, I think, it is the self-righteousness of an intelligent and innocent new generation in a world where my own generation is patently stupid and incompetent. They have been brought up on a literature of devastating criticism that has gone unanswered because there is no answer.

The philosophical words are "authenticity" and "commitment," from the existentialist vocabulary. And it cannot be denied that our dominant society is unusually inauthentic. Newspeak and double-talk[42] are the *lingua franca* of administrators, politicians, advertisers, and mass media. These people are not even lying; rather, there is an unbridgeable chasm between the statements made for systemic reasons or the image of the corporation and what is intended and actually performed. I have seen mature graduate-students crack up in giggles of anxiety listening to the Secretary of State expound our foreign policy with his usual patient good humor; when I questioned them afterward, some said that he was like a mechanical man, others

---

[41] Students for a Democratic Society was a student activist movement that represented the country's New Left. The organization developed and expanded rapidly in the mid-1960s before dissolving at its last convention in 1969. A faction of SDS formed the Weather Underground, identified by the FBI as a "domestic terrorist group."

[42] These terms were coined by George Orwell in his *1984*, and are discussed at great length in the "Appendix" of that novel. It specifically refers to the deliberately impoverished language promoted by the totalitarian state depicted in *1984*.

that he was demented. The trouble was that his personal aplomb was not related to his function and action; he was not engaged. And most campus blow-ups have been finally caused by administrators' animal inability to speak. The students have faithfully observed due process and manfully stated their case, but the administrators simply could not talk like human beings.

In principle, "commitment" proves authenticity. You must not merely talk but organize, collect money, burn your draft card,[43] go South and be shot at, go to jail. And the young eagerly commit themselves. However, a lasting commitment is hard to achieve. There are a certain number of causes that are pretty authentic and warrant engaging in: give blacks the vote, desegregate a hotel or bus, practice fair employment, commute Chessman's sentence to the gas chamber, abolish grading and get the CIA out of the university, get out of Vietnam, legalize marijuana and homosexuality, unionize the grape-pickers. But it is rarely the case that any particular authentic cause can really occupy the thought and energy of more than a few for more than a while. Students cool off and hop from issue to issue. Then some become angry at the backsliders; others foolishly try to prove that civil liberties, for instance, are not so "important" as black American civil rights, for instance, or that university reform is not so "important" as stopping the bombing of Hanoi. Others, disillusioned, sink into despair of human nature. And committed causes vanish from view at the June vacation, when the community disperses.

Shrewder psychologists among the young advocate getting involved only in what you "enjoy" and gravitate to, but this is a weak motive compared with indignation or justice.

---

[43] Compulsory active service in the armed forces, i.e. the draft, ended in 1973. The draft card was mailed to an individual notifying them of this commitment. At the time of Goodman's lecture, there were many rallies held where individuals openly "burned" their cards in protest to the war.

The bother is that, except with a few political or religious personalities, the students' commitments do not spring from their own vocations and life ambitions; and they are not related in a coherent program for the reconstruction of society. This is not the fault of the students. Most of the present young have unusually little sense of vocation—perhaps sixteen continuous years of doing lessons by compulsion is not a good way to find identity; and there *is* no acceptable program of reconstruction—nobody has spelled it out—only vague criteria. Pathetically, much "definite commitment" is a self-deceptive way of filling the void of sense of vocation and utopian politics. Black Americans, who are perforce really committed to their emancipation, notice this and say that their white allies are spiritually exploiting them.

It is a terrible period for the young to find vocation and identity. For most of the abiding human vocations and professions, arts and sciences, seem to them, and are, corrupt; law, business, the physical sciences, social work—these constitute the hated System. And higher education, both curriculum and professors, which ought to be helping them find themselves, also seems corrupt and part of the System. Students know that something is wrong in their schooling and they agitate for university reform, but since they do not know what new world they want to make, they do not know what to demand to be taught.

4

It is not the task of 20-year-olds to devise a coherent program of social reconstruction, to rethink the uses of technology and resources, methods of management, city planning, and international relations; and they rightly accuse us of not providing them a program to work for. A small minority, I think increasing, return to Marxism, but the Marxist theorists have also not thought of anything new and relevant to over-mature societies. Most radical students, in my observation, listen to Marxist ideological speeches with polite lack of interest, and are appalled by Marxist political bullying. On the other hand, they are disgusted with official anti-communism. By an inevitable backlash, since they think all American official speech is double-talk, they disbelieve that communist states are any worse than our own.

What the American young do know, being themselves pushed around, itemized, and processed, is that they have a right to a say in what affects them; that is, they believe in democracy, which they have to call "participatory democracy," to distinguish it from double-talk democracy. Poignantly, in their ignorance of American history, they do not recognize that they are Congregationalists, town-meeting democrats, Jeffersonians, populists.[44] But they know they want the opportunity to be responsible, to initiate and decide, instead of being mere personnel. Returning from their term overseas, the first thousand of the Peace Corps[45] unanimously agreed that exercising responsibility and initiative had been the most worthwhile part of their experience, and they complained that back home they would not have the opportunity. (Last year at Harvard more seniors opted for the Peace Corps than for business!)

The primary area for seeking democracy would be, one would imagine, the universities, for that is where the students are and are coerced. And the radical students, who we have seen are among the best academically, have worked for *Lernfreiheit*–freedom from grading, excessive examination, compulsory attendance at lectures, and prescribed subjects–and also for the ancient privilege of a say in

---

[44] The Jeffersonians believed in democracy and equality for the "yeoman farmer" and the "plain folk". They were antagonistic to the supposed aristocratic elitism of merchants and manufacturers. Above all, the Jeffersonians were devoted to the principles of Republicanism, especially civic duty and opposition to privilege, aristocracy and corruption.

[45] The Peace Corps is an American volunteer program run by the United States Government. The work is generally related to social and economic development.

designing the curriculum and evaluating the teaching. But unfortunately, as we have also seen, the majority of students do not care about higher education as such; they are in college for a variety of extrinsic reasons, from earning the degree necessary for getting a salary, to evading the draft. There is no mass base for university reform in the universities.

Mainly, instead of working in their own bailiwick, the radical students have sought participatory democracy for poor people, organizing rent strikes, marching for black American suffrage, opposing the welfare bureaucrats, and so forth. But again there is an inherent dilemma. Blacks claim, perhaps correctly, that middle-class whites cannot understand their problems, and if blacks are going to run their own show they have to dispense with white helpers. The present policy of the Student Non-Violent Coordinating Committee[46] is that black Americans must solve their own peculiar problems which are the only ones they care about and know anything about, and let their young white friends attend to changing the majority society. There is something in this. Certainly one would have expected northern radical students to get their heads broken in the cafeteria at the University of Mississippi, where they could talk with their peers face to face, as well as on the streets of country towns. And white southern liberals have desperately needed more support than they have gotten.

But pushed too far, separation consigns poor people to a second-class humanity. Some pressing problems are universal; the poor *must* care about them, e.g. the atom bombs. Many problems are grossly misconceived if looked at from a poor man's point of view; only a broad human point of view can save black Americans from agitating for exactly the wrong things, for example the

---

[46] The Student Nonviolent Coordinating Committee (SNCC) was one of the principal organizations of the American Civil Rights Movement in the 1960s. SNCC's major contribution was in its field work, organizing voter registration drives all over the South, especially in Georgia, Alabama, and Mississippi.

Educational Parks,[47] when what is needed in schooling is small human scale. Also, there is something spurious in the separation, for a poor minority in a highly technological and middle-class society will not engineer the housing and manufacture the cars, etc., that they intend to use. Finally, in fact the blacks are, perhaps unfortunately, much more American than African-American. Especially in the North, they aspire to the same American package, though it makes even less sense for them than for anybody else. The black American sub-culture that is talked up has about the same value as the adolescent sub-culture, with which it shares many traits in common; it has vitality and it does not add up to humanity.

As in other periods of moral change, only the young aristocrats and the intellectuals can *afford* to be disillusioned and profoundly radical.

In their own action organizations, the young are almost fanatically opposed to top-down direction. In several remarkable cases, gifted and charismatic student leaders have stepped down because their influence had become too strong. By disposition, without benefit of history, they have reinvented anarchist federation and a kind of Luxemburgian belief in spontaneous insurrection from below. They tend to the kind of nonviolent resistance in which each one makes his own moral decision about getting his head broken, rather than submitting to rigid discipline. If there is violence, they will surely be guerillas rather than an organized army.

All this, in my opinion, probably makes them immune to take-over by centralists like the Marxists. When Trotskyists,[48] for instance,

---

[47] The federal Elementary and Secondary Educational Act of 1965 put forward the provision to recycle the site of the 1964 World's Fair in Queens for one of these Educational Parks, serving up to 25, 000 students.

[48] A follower of Leon Trotsky, who was one of the founding members of Soviet communism. His politics differed sharply from those of Stalinism, most prominently in opposing (Stalin's) Socialism in One Country, which he argued was a break with proletarian internationalism.

infiltrate an organization and try to control it, the rest go home and activity ceases. When left to their own improvisation, however, the students seem surprisingly able to mount quite massive efforts, using elaborate techniques of communication and expert sociology. By such means they will never get power. But indeed, they do not want power, they want meaning.

The operative idea in participatory democracy is decentralizing, to multiply the number who are responsible, initiate and decide. Is this idea viable? (I have discussed the question at length in *People or Personnel,* arguing for a mixed system of central and decentral management by state, corporations, cooperatives, and independents.)

In principle, there are two opposite ways of decentralizing: either by dividing over-centralized organizations where it can be shown that decentral organization is more efficient in economic, social, and human costs—or at least not too inefficient; or by creating new small enterprises to fulfill needs that big organizations neglect or only pretend to fulfill. Obviously the first of these, to cut the present structures down to human size, is not in the power of students; but it happens that it does require a vast amount of empirical research and academic analysis, to find if, where, and how it is feasible. In the current American style, there is no such research and analysis, and on 150 campuses I have urged students to work on such problems, in business and engineering, education and communications, science and municipal administration. The students seem fascinated, but I do not know if they are coming across. (To say it wryly, there is an excellent organization called Students for a Democratic Society, but it is not enough evident that they are *students* for a democratic society.)

The opposite way of decentralizing, by creating new enterprises, better suits the student zeal for direct action, and they have applied it with a lot of energy and some inventiveness. It has been called "parallel development." Typically, students have set up a dozen little "free universities" in or next to established institutions, to teach in a more personal way and to deal with contemporary subjects that are not yet standard (e.g. "Castro's Cuba," "The Psychedelic Experience," "Sensitivity Training," "Theater of Participation").[49] Some of these courses are "action sociology," like organizing labor or community development. Students have established a couple of neighborhood radio stations, to broadcast local news and propaganda, and to give poor people a chance to talk into a microphone. They have set up parallel community projects to combat the welfare bureaucracy and channelize real needs and grievances. In the South they have helped form "freedom" political machines since the established machines are lily-white.[50] They have offered to organize international service projects as an alternative to serving in the army. (As yet I have not heard of any feasible attempts at productive co-operatives or urban "intentional communities," and students do not seem to be interested in rural reconstruction.)

Looked at coldly, such parallel projects are pitifully insignificant and doomed to pass away like little magazines. Yet they are a thrilling revival of the seemingly dead spirit of American populism: get out from under the thumb of the barons and do it yourself. In my opinion the important step is the first one, to prove that such things are possible at all; then there is no telling how far they will go. There is a good hope for bringing to life many of our institutions by surrounding them with human enterprises, like a cambium or growing layer. The most telling criticism of an overgrown institution is a simpler one that works better.

---

[49] It is an attempt to use theatre within a political system to create a truer form of democracy. Augusto Boal developed this form of theatre in the early 1960s and its central technique known as the "spect-actor" (a spectator-turned-actor). See Boal's *Legislative Theatre*, 1998.

[50] See note 45 for the SNCC's role in organizing voter registration drives.

This was the educational vision of John Dewey[51] sixty years ago, of an industrial society continually democratically renewed by its young, freely educated and learning by doing. Progressive education, free-spirited but practical, was a typical populist conception. And the student movement can be regarded as progressive education at the college and graduate school level, where it begins to be indistinguishable from vocation and politics. It is the antithesis of a mandarin establishment and the social engineering that we now call education. Maybe this time around it will work.

So, describing American radical youth, and to a degree many other American youth, we have noticed their solidarity based on community rather than ideology, their style of direct and frank confrontation and personal contact, their democratic inclusiveness and aristocratic confidence careless of status, caste, or getting ahead, their selectivity and somewhat defiance of the affluent standard of living, their striving to be authentic and committed to their causes rather than merely belonging, their determination to have a say and their refusal to be pushed around or processed as standard items, their extreme distrust of top-down direction, their disposition to anarchist organization and direct action, their disillusion with the system of institutions and their belief that they can carry on major social functions in improvised parallel enterprises. Some of these traits, in my opinion, are natural to all unspoiled young people, but all of them are certainly in contradiction to the dominant organization of American society.

By and large this is as yet the disposition of a minority of the young, but it is the only articulate disposition that has emerged, and it has continuously emerged for the past ten years. It is a response not merely to "issues," like Civil Rights or Vietnam, but to deeply

---

[51] John Dewey (1859–1952) was an American philosopher whose ideas have been influential in education and social reform. Dewey was an important early developer of the philosophy of pragmatism and one of the founders of functional psychology.

rooted defects in our present system and it will have an influence in the future. Those who think it is the usual "generational revolt," that will be absorbed as the students get "older and wiser," are whistling in the dark. If it is not taken seriously and compounded with, the result will be ever deepening alienation and, ultimately, worse disruption.

The empty style of our society pervades most functions and institutions. In recent books I have described it in education and in our manner of social organization. In the next two lectures let me single out how we think about scientific technology and urbanization.

It is becoming common among social philosophers to treat the progress of science and technology as if it now goes on by itself and determines, like the Marxist "relations of production" everything else, but it is even less dependent on human choice. Whatever men wish, the independent development of scientific technology will shape the future. In more drastic versions of the theory, technology has already changed man into a product of itself, or man has become one special function in the technical system.

To Jacques Ellul,[52] for instance, the American "empty society" can be more simply defined as an inevitable result of our high technology where, in his words, "work implies an absence of man, whereas previously it implied a presence." He means that a few motions of human labor and brains are selected and used mechanically and the rest must be deleted as an interference. (I have laid stress, rather, on the fact that large groups of people are excluded altogether, rather than exploited.) The controlling social organization, to which I have attributed independent influence, is to Ellul nothing but a function of technology itself, which in its essence standardizes, swallows up every case, and controls. And the populist

---

[52] Jacques Ellul (1912–1994) was a French philosopher, law professor, sociologist, lay theologian, and Christian anarchist. The dominant theme of his 58 books has been the threat to human freedom and Christian faith created by modern technology.

and libertarian counter-forces that I described in my last lecture are to him whistling in the dark; he would say they are like his own complaints, "the work of some miserable intellectual who balks at technical progress. What good is it to pose questions of motive? Technique exists because it is technique."

Your own Marshall McLuhan of the University of Toronto pursues the same theme less pessimistically. He holds that the technical style of communications alters the nature of human perception and thought. It makes little difference, he says, what message or entertainment is broadcast on television, or whether the airways are a free forum or are regimented by monopolies, for the effect on human nature has already occurred because of the electronics medium itself. There is no point in making value judgments, and Professor McLuhan claims, at least in his delightful lectures, that he is morally neutral. (I think he is privately more disturbed.)

For Pierre Teilhard de Chardin, however, the new knowledge and technique constitute no less than a leap forward in organic evolution, transcending humanity as we have known it. Essentially, we now inhabit the Noösphere, the world-wide network of exchange of scientific information. Behavior no longer springs from animal humors, the personal conflict of passion and reason, or the politics of groups, but from the decision of the giant intellectual spirit. As a pious Christian, Teilhard de Chardin is enthusiastic about our new state of being, which is imbued with divine love. I am bemused at the nature of the love given or received, as either eros or agape,[53] by what seem to be information-retrieval computers, but no doubt I fail to understand.

Here, then, are three strong minds who see essentially the same phenomenon, the system of scientific technology brooding free and

---

[53] Greek terms for love. Agape being the "ideal" form.

determining the future, though they evaluate it differently as horrible, neutral, or blessed.

Yet the gross history of the past hundred years does not reveal this free floating technology. Scientific technology has certainly affected with its products, processes, and method most human beings and nearly every human function; in large areas it has created an artificial landscape and altered the balance of species; it has gotten off the planet and may destroy a good part of life on the planet. But invariably, in its quantity and in its direction of development, scientific technology has been in the employ of familiar human motives: either convenience, health, and excitement, or profits, power, and the aggrandizement of persons or groups. It has not been independent. On the contrary, it can be shown that the organization of recent scientific technology has, by and large, moved *away* from the traditional research autonomy of science and the principle of efficiency of technology, and under political, military, and economic control. If they were organized in their own terms, science and technology would be very differently organized. At present there is a waste of scientists' time and brains, and engineers are not allowed to decide like real professionals. And the increasing moral and ritual drives to standardization, rationalization, control, and self-control—what Max Weber called the Protestant Ethic—have not, in my opinion, been mainly due to technical routine but to new psychological obsessions to ward off insecurity, and compulsions to identify with power. People submit to inhuman routine out of fear and helplessness. And such routine is *not* of the essence of scientific technology. In the past both science and technology progressed better without such rituals, and they would do so now.

The present submissive state of scientific technology is a sad betrayal of the promise of independent scientific technology dreamed of by Thomas Huxley, Kropotkin, Veblen, John Dewey, Buckminster Fuller. They thought of science as humble, brave, and austere, and of technology as circumspect, neat, and serviceable. Working by its own morale, scientific technology should by now have simplified life rather than complicated it, emptied the environment rather than cluttered it, and educated an inventive and skillful generation rather than a conformist and inept one. It is the same with the effect of the technological development of communications, which Marshall McLuhan makes much of. Norbert Wiener[54] used to point out that repetition of communication just increases the noise; in general, he said, there is more new information in a good poem than in a scientific report. Then, if our electronics media, and printing media, were doing their job, there would be less brainwashing and less gabble altogether; and Americans would not be spending six hours a day watching television and learning new habits of perception.

Jacques Ellul is mistaken about us miserable intellectuals. We complain not because we balk at technical progress but because we are disappointed in it.

2

Since I intend to complain about the present morale of scientific technology, let me first make clear what I do not complain of. Science *is* autonomous, because knowledge must be pursued for its own sake as part of the human adventure. Despite the risks involved, for instance in nuclear physics, most people honor this claim. I do. Also, technology is grounded in the human principle that you must give a workman the best tool, otherwise he is degraded. Despite the disruption sometimes involved, for instance in automation, most

---

[54] Norbert Wiener is regarded as the originator of cybernetics, a formalization of the notion of feedback, with many implications for engineering, systems control, computer science, biology, philosophy, and the organization of society. See his *The Human Use of Human Beings.*

people are not Luddite and do not oppose technological advance. I do not.

Apart from these basic principles, however, the meaning of both science and technology has changed radically in the past fifty years. The often repeated statement that there are more scientists now alive than existed in all previous time ought to put us on the alert. How do these new multitudes of scientists take themselves? How are they in the world?

The present orthodox philosophy of scientific technology is that there is something called pure science or basic research which is morally neutral (except for the drive toward knowledge). Its inquiries may or may not lead to anything useful. Useful findings are "applied" and become part of the system of technology.

This is a peculiar position, and quite untraditional. What is neutral science? What is "applied" science? There *is* a difference between science and technology. It is reasonable to make the Aristotelian distinction between science as an act of wonder, disinterested curiosity, and esthetic construction, and technique as empirical rules of thumb for efficient practice; but, especially since the Renaissance, natural philosophers[55] would not have made a big deal of such a distinction. Every theory has operations and apparatus; and a *reasoned* machine, like a steam engine or a storage battery, is a model of its theory, it is not an "application." It is the machine, not the theory, that is "applied" or put to use; this is a matter of choice and capitalization, not of technology as such. In fact, of course, science and technology have rarely gone separate ways anyway. It would be odd if they had. Agriculture, domestication of animals, measurement, building, machinery, navigation, transportation, communication, politics, war, pedagogy, medicine, all abound in controlled experiments that invite observation and testing;

---

[55] An earlier term for a scientist.

their difficulties and errors lead to new questions; new apparatus makes new theory. Contrariwise, any natural discovery is bound to be tried out; a model is built if only as a toy; and natural philosophers have always put their wits to work for industry, war, and medicine.

What is striking is that the doctrine of pure science and its moral neutrality[56] always comes to the fore when scientists are assigned an official status and become salaried or subsidized, as in the German universities in the 19th century or in America today. It looks like an attempt, on the part of the scientists, to affirm their identity and protect themselves against officious interference by managers; but it is also, I am afraid, a self-deception and a hoax on the public. In America at present the great bulk of the billions of dollars for science is for research on extrinsically chosen problems, or even on particular products. A large part of the training of scientists in the universities is toward rather narrow technological expertness. Of nearly $20 billion[57] marked for Research and Development, more than 90% is actually devoted to last-stage designing of hardware for production. Corporations mark up prices 1,000% in order, they say, to pay for basic research, but much of the research is to bypass other firms' patents. It is hard to credit that this kind of science is disinterested, and that promoters are not using the prestige of science as a talking-point.

It is taken for granted that amazing new developments will, if possible, at once be sequestered for military use and sometimes be made secret. Lasers will be death rays. The adventure of space will end in orbiting missile sites. The chief use of drugs that influence behavior will be to paralyze an enemy's will to resist. Anthropology

---

[56] The evolutionary biologist, Richard Lewontin, discusses the notion of "neutrality" of scientists at length in his *Biology as Ideology* (1991).
[57] According to the U.S. National Science Foundation, the overall spending on R&D conducted in the United States was $398 billion (current dollars) in 2008, up from $373 billion in 2007.

is for counter-insurgency in primitive countries. And even the benevolent dolphins are to be trained as kamikaze submarines. Unfortunately this is not a caricature. Then it is dismaying to hear dedicated scientists explain that they are allowed perfect freedom to do restricted-publication research, and that any theoretical problem is indifferently good for the progress of science. The simplest explanation of the proposition that "there are more scientists alive today than existed up to now" is that business-as-usual has co-opted science. It is not that our society has become scientific, but that to be a "scientist" has become one of the acceptable roles.

Make an historical contrast. During the heroic age of modern science, say from the 16th through the 18th centuries, natural philosophers believed, uncritically and perhaps naively, that they directly confronted the nature of things and were in a kind of dialogue with Nature with a capital N. Each man was solitarily engaged in this open dialogue which might lead in any direction and hopefully surprisingly. But since all were engaged in a common enterprise on the frontier of knowledge, they eagerly communicated with one another, by publication, academies, depositing theses in university libraries, and enormous correspondence by letter. (Theorists of anarchism point to the sublime progress of modern science as a triumph of almost perfect co-ordination without top-down management.) The duty of publication to allow others to replicate the experiment became part of the definition of science; by it one became honored as the first. One is puzzled as to what restricted "scientific" information can mean. Does "replicable" mean "replicable by those cleared by the FBI"?

During the heroic period, science was not the social orthodoxy. Indeed, a disproportionate number of the natural philosophers were exploring forbidden territory and publishing defiantly. They were not getting any grants. Their image was rough and morose or moonstruck and bumbling. Their claim to freedom of inquiry was grounded not in a formal distinction about role but in a civil conflict about content; this confirmed their solidarity as a rebellious band. They were not morally neutral, nor was Nature morally neutral. Nature was wonderful or horrible or fascinating; she was surely beyond ordinary human uses, but abounding in moral as well as practical lessons for human betterment.

In their hearts, I am sure, many scientists still belong to the ancient band—just as many academics still vote with Abelard. Sometimes a great scientist talks the old language. Old-fashioned moralists hanker after a "natural ethics" or a "scientific way of life." But the official position is quite otherwise. Science is no longer a dialogue with Nature but a system of expanding knowledge that is self-contained and self-correcting, something like Hegel's progressive Absolute Idea.[58] It is to this system that scientists are dedicated and which they serve with a special method practiced with considerable formal scrupulosity, so that it sometimes seems to be the correct method rather than the content that constitutes scientific truth. Rather than banded individuals, scientists have become an organized priesthood, and their system has become the major orthodoxy of modern society; it is the system of ideas that everybody—including myself—believes, whether or not one knows anything about it. The popular feeling about it contains both superstitious reverence and superstitious fear, and the current mass-education in science, we shall see, does not allay these. By and large, however, laymen are convinced that the progress of science will increase human happiness.

---

[58] It is Hegel's account of how being is ultimately comprehensible as an all-inclusive whole. Hegel asserted that in order for the thinking subject (human reason or consciousness) to be able to know its object (the world) at all, there must be in some sense an identity of thought and being. Otherwise, the subject would never have access to the object and we would have no certainty about any of our knowledge of the world.

The shift of emphasis from an open dialogue of morose or bumbling men with surprising Nature to an elite service to a progressive self-correcting system of knowledge has been accompanied by immense changes in the social organization of science, the role of the scientist, and the personal engagement of the man in the role. There is now less use for individual genius and hunch, and less opportunity for a personal ethical choice of a field of search as peculiarly fascinating, congenial, or "good." The issue is not, let me make it clear, whether the field is benevolent or useful, for it has often been the hallmark of scientific genius to research the senseless, the apparently trivial, the pathological. But I doubt that an older-style scientist paid attention to what *he* considered indifferent. His work was suffused with himself—and it is my Wordsworthian[59] bias that scientists and artists, formed by their disinterested conversation with meaning, are usually good people. When a study is pursued as indifferently scientific, however, it is likely that extrinsic purposes will dictate the direction that is taken. Inevitably there is pressure for pay-off results rather than the wandering dialogue with surprise. A scientist becomes personnel, pursuing the goals of the organization.

More fatefully, as a great successful institution, the system of knowledge has become interlocked with the other great institutions of society, and the dominant style takes over. But this style was not devised for open dialogue with surprise; it was devised for cash-accounting, tax collection, military discipline, logistics, and mass-manufacture. Yet bureaucratic methods, it is believed, must somehow be appropriate to science too. Committees *must* be able to evaluate "projects." There *must* be profiles of gifted persons to support, and there *must* be university courses relevant to training others. Scientific thinking must be able to be parcelled out for

---

[59] Goodman is referring to the English Romantic poet, William Wordsworth. The Romantic poets are known for their suspicion of the scientific establishment. One Romantic poet, William Blake, often compiled "Bacon, Newton & Lock" into his notion of the unholy trinity.

efficient division of labor, and discoveries must occur on schedule: basic research, application, development, shaping up for production. With enough capital, one can mount a crash program and break through. To be serviceable, excellent scientists become administrators. Grant-getters, who are clever about the forms, become scientists. Corporations become impresarios for scientists. Scientific brains from other countries are bought up to work in the American style on American problems, seriously depoverishing their own peoples and precluding the development of various schools of thought. In the end, unless an hypothesis involves big cash, its author cannot afford to pursue it, though he used to love it.

The rationalization is ready to hand. Modern science *requires* big capital and big organization: take cyclotrons, moon shots, statistical surveys, universal information-retrieval. These are now science *par excellence*. There has been a re-definition. By-passing the experience of nearly four hundred years, the method of observation, analysis, deduction, and crucial experiment, we have amazingly come back full circle to the bureaucratic system of Bacon's *Novum Organum*,[60] a dragnet of facts, stored, retrieved, and computed.

It is hard to know whether the corporate style of research is really the best one, for it tends to be self-proving. If brainy people agree to operate in this manner, they are not operating in some other manner and we do not know what they would be producing. Yet there is a curious body of evidence compiled by the Anti-Trust Committee of the United States Senate that shows rather overwhelmingly that in recent decades, even in practical Research

---

[60] Francis Bacon has been called the father of empiricism. In his *Novum Organum (1620),*Bacon's ambition was to create a new system of philosophy to replace that of Aristotle, and it has inspired later scientists, rationalists and materialists. His works established and popularised inductive methodologies for scientific inquiry, often called the *Baconian method*, or simply the scientific method.

and Development, the majority of significant advances have *not* come from big corporations and big universities, and have not been sponsored by foundations and government; they have still come from lonely (and often rejected) individuals, random amateur inventors, partnerships, tiny firms where the scientists, technicians, and craftsmen have a chance to talk to one another. One would expect this to be still more so in pure science.

Let me make myself clear once again. I am not opposed to heavy subsidies for science. It is one of the few things that make it worthwhile to be human; no price can be set on it. But, like art, perhaps science is hard to buy directly. Perhaps the best we can do is provide a decent society in which people can be themselves and children can grow up with their lively curiosity not too stultified. By definition, anything radically new must seem far-fetched except to its innovator. Certainly, as public policy–if only to increase the general cultivation–I would decentralize subsidies for science as widely as possible rather than, as we do, letting the money go to a few managers.

3

The morality of technology has also suffered a sea-change. Historically, the main origin of technology, in the work of craftsmen, miners, navigators, etc., provided a ready check on utility, efficiency, costs, and unforeseen effects. A secondary but important origin, in the natural experiments of Medieval and Renaissance alchemists and magicians, and perhaps physicians, provided no such check; the archetypal story is *The Sorcerer's Apprentice*. But therefore these groups had a strong ethical code, to permit only white magic, and prescribing Christian virtue as the priceless ingredient of the Philosopher's Stone. The Black Magician, like our Mad Scientist, was a villain for popular tragedy.

But even with the Industrial Revolution and the capitalization of machinery finally for cash profits rather than any other purpose, the market itself provided a check on the cheapness of the process and the utility of the products, although of course the whole system was notoriously careless of social costs and remote effects like enclosure, slums, air pollution, slag heaps, and the exhaustion of resources.

In principle, the discipline of Political Economy was, and is, supposed to regulate costs and benefits so as to guarantee the general good. In this discipline, the use and extent of a technology are subject to prudence, including safety, caution because of the possibility of unforeseen disadvantages, forethought to prevent over-commitment, and concern for the shape and function of the whole.

The history has been different. Political Economy did not devote itself to these matters but to the Gross National Product measured in cash; its advice was, and is, how to maximize technological growth to increase the abstract number of goods and services, whatever their quality or mutual contradictions. The check of the market has been weakened by subsidies, cost-plus contracts, monopolies, price-fixing, advertising, and the ignorance of consumers. And the various technologies increasingly interlock and depend on one another in a vast and recondite system, so that it has become fantastically difficult even for experts to decide what is by and large useful, cheap, or even safe. No one at all can trace the remote effects. And the control of the systems of technology, and of the systems of systems, is lodged in managers who finally are not interested in efficiency, not to speak of prudence. They are not in business for technical or citizenly reasons.

There ceases to be a morality of technique at all. A technician is hired to execute a detail of a program handed down to him. Apart from honestly trying to make his detail work, he is not entitled to criticize the program itself, in terms of its efficiency, common sense, beauty, effect on the community, or human scale. If management is not concerned with these either, a technician must often lend his wits to ludicrous contradictions. Cars are designed to go faster than it is safe to drive; food is processed to take out the nourishment; housing is expertly engineered to destroy neighborhoods; weapons are stockpiled that only a maniac would use. The ultimate of irresponsibility is that the engineer is not allowed to know what he is making, and we have had this too.

The interlocking of systems of technology without the direct check of personal acquaintance and use and political prudence creates a series of booby traps. Human scale may be quite disregarded, the time and energy that people actually have, the space they need to move in, and the rhythm or randomness with which they best operate. As the engineers design, we move, or sometimes can't move. Facilities are improved, but during the transition everybody is inconvenienced, and by the time the facility is completed it may be obsolescent. Fast trips are made possible by jet, but they prove to chop up our lives, to involve longer trips to airports and more waiting in terminals, so we have less free time. Business machines are installed and there is no longer any person from whom to get information or service for one's particular case. Cities spread so far that one can't get out of them; the country is deserted, so it is inefficient to provide means to get to it. Immense printing presses and other means of communication are devised, but to warrant such an investment of capital requires a mass audience, and it becomes hard to publish a serious book or transmit a serious message.

This sounds like chaos and modern life pretty nearly is. Apart from the cure of infectious diseases, some public services, and some household and farm equipment, there have been few recent advances in technique that have not proved to be a mixed bag in actual convenience. The great advantages, on balance, that came from universalizing basic conveniences or necessities, like electricity or water-supply, do not necessarily occur when massifying comforts and luxuries. The moral advantages, of enriched opportunity, are largely delusory. New opportunities do not make time available to enjoy them, and the chance for choice works out as superficial acquaintance and confusion. The marvels of fable, like flying through the air and seeing at a distance, have not proved so beautiful in reality. It is not hard to fantasize a use of our high technology that would be neat, uncomplicated, rich, and educative; but it is significant that Utopian writers have stopped fantasizing in this direction. The fact remains that countries with a fifth or a tenth of our available technology have a way of life that is as good or better. I do not mean by this argument that we ought to cut back our technology, for human beings are bound to try out everything; but there *is* a problem here that we have no right to disregard as we do.

There is a new technological instrument of Political Economy that, ideally, could follow up some of the bewildering remote effects of innovation and detect the contradictions before they occur. This is computing costs and benefits. But it would have to be used authentically, focusing on what happens to people rather than on the convenience of the programmer or the aggrandizement of his system. Actual examples, in city planning, welfare, education, and foreign policy, have not been promising. They tend to omit from the equations factors that are unknown or stubbornly existing but excessively complicated, like individual differences, history, anomie, esthetics, the changeableness of policy. Then, though wise and impartial, the computer cannot give its best advice, which might often be: Not safe! Do not over-commit! Take it easy! Make it human! Instead, on the basis of puerile theories the programmers compute hard-nosed facts—"hard" facts are those with numbers attached—and bull through solutions to which human beings with the flexibility and fortitude that, God bless them, they have, adjust as best they can. The theories are thus confirmed.

4

Let me suggest two kinds of remedies to restore morale to scientific technology.

The first is to judge technology directly in terms of the moral criteria appropriate to it as a branch of practical philosophy. (How odd it is that today this obvious proposal has an odd ring!) Consider a possible list of criteria: Utility, Efficiency, Comprehensibility, Repairability, Flexibility, Amenity, Relevance, Modesty. By utility I mean, for instance, not pushing brand-name variety that makes no practical difference, whether in cars or drugs; not building obsolescence into expensive machines as if they were children's toys. By efficiency, I mean especially not over-riding the competence of technicians for the demands of the system; not disregarding thrift merely for convenience of administration—for instance, radical decentralization would often save on costs, as well as giving more control to those who do the work. By comprehensibility of design and concern for repairability we might alleviate the growing ineptitude of users and their bondage to repair-men and corporation service-stations. By flexibility we might stave off the increasingly frequent disasters that occur when interlocking systems of technology break down as a whole because of stoppage in a part; we might ease the entry of small enterprises and new regions into the economy. By amenity I mean concern for the whole range of feelings, not trivia like getting rid of billboards but the frayed nerves of traffic congestion, the destruction of cities by freeways, the chewing up of landscape for quick profits and transient convenience; not breeding out the taste and maturity of food for the convenience of processors and packagers. By relevance I mean concern for human scale, the time, size, energy, need for space of actual people, rather than calculating efficiency in abstract units of time, space, and energy. By modesty I mean not looming larger than a function warrants; caution about hasty commitment and over-commitment which by now have given us several generations of slums of engineering and piles of junk.

Another valuable consideration is to check competition in technology when an enterprise reaches a size and expense that makes it a natural monopoly that should be regulated in the public interest or nationalized. At present, I think, this applies especially to automating, where it is absurd to duplicate immense concentrations of tools—though it might be wise radically to decentralize the programming. It certainly applies to the crazy competition in exploring space.

Such a moral program is, I say, obvious; yet it is revolutionary and beyond our present political means. We can legislate, and exact penalties for, hazard, dishonest claims, and malpractice, but not for slovenliness, childish gluttony, callousness about the community, and indecency. Then the public becomes resigned. Nevertheless, in my opinion, a lot would be accomplished if technicians would take the lead and insist on acting like professionals. Common people would follow their lead and find political means. It is endlessly amazing how people spring back to life and good instincts if they see a glimmer of hope; there is a dramatic reversal in the opinion polls.

5

Much could be accomplished also by a different kind of mass education in science. I agree with the current wisdom that in a world pervaded with scientific technology, a great part of the curriculum must be scientific. The question is for what purpose and how. At present, there is some effort to teach the excitement and beauty of science and natural truth, and to get great men to give the TV lessons; this is laudable. But the chief purpose of most recent curriculum reform seems to me to be wrong-headed: it is to process Ph.D.'s or even to educate creative scientists; and the method is to teach the latest findings. The time of the vast majority who are not going on to scientific careers is wasted. Yet it is likely that most of those who are scientifically gifted will follow their bent anyway, quicker than they can in standard courses. We really do not know how to educate for creative genius. And it is not the case, as is claimed, that in a high technology average workers need extensive scientific schooling; on the contrary, a few weeks to a year on the job, rather than years of lessons, is still the best way to train adequate low-level technicians.

Entirely neglected in the present curriculum, however, is what science *is,* as a way of being in the world. For instance, its austerity and honesty. For this, it is worse than useless for the average student to learn answers for the College Board examinations. This turns the whole thing into an abstraction or a hoax. The student ought instead to be scrupulously reporting what happened in his laboratory, why his experiment did *not* "work out"–of course, it has worked out some way or other.

There should be heavy emphasis on becoming at home in the actual technology, making model machines and learning to repair intelligently the usual standard machines. This was the scientific program of classical progressive education fifty years ago, to make critical and self-reliant users in an industrial society, to restore the sense of causal control of things rather than feeling powerless among things.

As part of social studies, a major subject should be the economics, politics, and organization of science and technology. I do not see any way for the average citizen to be able to judge the substantive issues relevant to the vast sums for research and development, medicine, space exploration, and technical training; but it would be helpful if he understood the interests and politics involved.

With regard to one area of science, however, it is essential that citizens do learn to judge the substantive issues. This is human ecology, combining physical science, physical and mental hygiene, sociology, and political economy, to analyze problems of urbanism, transportation, pollution, degenerative disease, mental disease, pesticides, indiscriminate use of antibiotics and other powerful drugs, and so forth. These matters are too important to be delegated to experts.

6

A few years ago, C. P. Snow[61] created a stir by speaking of the chasm between "two cultures," that of the scientists and that of the humanists. Since we live in times dominated by scientific technology, he castigated the humanists especially for not knowing the other language. The point of this lecture has been that Sir Charles posed the issue wrongly. There is only one culture; and probably the scientific technologists have betrayed it most. Science, the dialogue with the unknown, is itself one of the humanities; and technology, practical efficiency, is a part of moral philosophy. Scientific technology has become isolated by becoming subject to the empty system of power: excluding, expanding, controlling. The remedy is for scientists and technicians to reassert their own proper principles and for ordinary people to stop being superstitious and to reassert their own control over their environment. Then there will be communication again.

---

[61] Sir Charles Percy Snow (1905–1980) was an English physicist and novelist. He is best known for his series of novels known collectively as *Strangers and Brothers*, and for "The Two Cultures," a 1959 lecture in which he laments the gulf between scientists and "literary intellectuals".

URBANIZATION AND
RURAL RECONSTRUCTION

I started the last lecture by pointing out how the present style of technology is regarded as an autonomous cause of history. It is even more so with urbanization. It is as if by a law of Nature—the favored metaphor is that the City is a Magnet—that by 1990 75% of the Americans will live in dense metropolitan areas.[62] At present only about 6% are listed as rural.

Yet, first of all, the urbanization is not a necessity of technology. On the contrary, the thrust of modern technology, e.g. electricity, power tools, automobiles, distant communication, and automation, would seem to be disurbanization, dispersal of population and industry: this was the thinking of Marx and Engels, Kropotkin, Patrick Geddes, Frank Lloyd Wright, and other enthusiasts of scientific technology.

The urbanization is not a necessity of population growth. In fact, with the bankruptcy of small farming, vast beautiful regions have been depopulating and sometimes returning to swamp. American growth is supposed to level off, in fifty years, at 300 million, not a crowded number for such a big area. Yet the cities already show signs of overpopulation. They do not provide adequate city services and probably cannot provide them; they are vulnerable to urban catastrophes that might destroy thousands; it is prohibitively costly to live decently in them; and, in my opinion,

---

[62] As of 2011, 84 percent of the United States' inhabitants live in suburban and urban areas, but cities occupy only 10 percent of the country's landmass. Rural areas occupy the remaining 90 percent (Yen, Hope (2011-07-28). "Rural US Disappearing? Population Share Hits Low." *Associated Press*. Retrieved 2011-11-25).

though this is hard to prove, the crowding is already more than is permissible for mental health and normal growing up.

But it is as with the misuse of technology: the urbanization is mainly due not to natural or social-psychological causes, but to political policy and an economic style careless of social costs and even money costs. Certainly cities are magnets, of excitement and high culture, markets, centers of administration, and arenas to make careers; but these classical functions of cities of 100,000, capitals of their regions or nations, do not explain our sprawling agglomerations of many millions with no environment at all—Metropolitan New York City has 15 million,[63] and most people cannot get out of it. In general, magnet or no magnet, average people have been content to remain in the provinces and poor people never leave the land, unless they are driven out by some kind of enclosure system that makes it impossible to earn a living. Especially today, when the great American cities are morally and physically less and less attractive, while the towns and farms, equipped with TV, cars, and small machines that really pay off in the country, are potentially more and more attractive.

Like the rest of our interlocking system, the American system of enclosure has been an intricate complex. National farm subsidies have favored big plantations which work in various combinations with national chain grocers who now sell 70% of the food—100 companies more than 50%. Chains and processors merge. The chains and processors have used the usual tactics to undercut independents and co-operatives. In the cities, Federally financed urban renewal has bulldozed out of existence small vegetable stores and grocers, who are replaced by the chains. Shopping centers on new subsidized highways bypass villages and neighborhoods. Guaranteed by Federal mortgages, real estate promoters transform farmland into suburbs. Farmers' markets disappear from the cities. As rural regions depopulate, railroads discontinue service, with the approval of the Interstate Commerce Commission. Rural schools are

---

[63] As of 2010, the population of Metro NYC is 22,085,649.

encouraged to degenerate, and land-grant colleges change their curricula toward urban occupations. The Army and Navy recruit apace among displaced farmboys (as they do also among city black Americans and Spanish-Americans).

All this, which sounds like Oliver Goldsmith and Wordsworth, is rationalized by saying, as usual, that it is efficient. One farmer can now feed thirty people. Yet strangely, though most of the farmers are gone and the take of the remaining farmers indeed tends to diminish every year, the price of food is *not* cheaper, it is about the same. The difference goes to the processors, packagers, transporters, and middle-men. (Of course, with the present war-time inflation, food prices have risen spectacularly; but again, a disproportionate amount of the rise is due to processing and distribution.) These operate in the established style. That is, the urbanization and rural depopulation is not technical nor economic but political. The remarkable increase in technical efficiency could just as well produce rural affluence or a co-operative society of farmers and consumers.

It has certainly not been technically efficient to bulldoze the garden land of the missions of Southern California into freeways, aircraft factories, and suburbs choked by smog, and then to spend billions of public money to irrigate deserts, robbing water from neighboring regions. The destruction of California is probably our worst example of bad ecology, but it is all of a piece with the destruction of the fish and trees, the excessive use of pesticides, the pollution of the streams, the strip-mining of the land.

Of course, the galloping urbanization has been worldwide and it is most devastating in the so-called underdeveloped countries which cannot afford such blunders. Here the method of enclosure is more brutal. Typically, my country or some other advanced nation introduces a wildly inflationary standard, e.g. a few jobs at $70 a week when the average cash income of a peon[64] is $70 a year. If only to maintain their self-respect, peasants flock to the city where there

---

[64] A person held in servitude to work off debts or other obligations. According to a broadcast on Al Jezeera (Riz Khan; Aug. 02/09), there were 16, 000 "peons" in the U.S.

are no jobs for them; they settle around it in shanty-towns,[65] and die of cholera. They used to be poor but dignified and fed, now they are urbanized, degraded, and dead. Indeed, a striking contrast between the 18th-century enclosures and our own is that the dark Satanic mills needed the displaced hands, whereas we do not need unskilled labor. So along with our other foreign aid, we will have to bring literacy and other parts of the Great Society.

In the United States, though we collect the refugees in slums, we do not permit them to die of starvation or cholera. But I am again bemused at the economics of the welfare procedure. For instance, first, for 60 years, by a mercantilism worthy of George III, we destroyed Puerto Rican agriculture and prevented an industrialism solidly based at the bottom; then recently we allowed 800,000 Puerto Ricans—a majority with some rural background—to settle in New York City, the most expensive and morally strange possible environment, rather than bribing them to disperse. When share-cropping failed in the South, rather than subsidizing subsistence farming and making a try at community development, we give relief-money and social-work in Chicago and Los Angeles. Take it at its crudest level: if the cheapest urban public housing costs $20,000[66] a unit to build, and every city has a housing shortage, would it not be better to give farmers $1,000 a year for twenty years, just for rent, to stay home and drink their own water?

2

Partly our urban troubles spring from no planning, partly from just the planning that there is. When concrete observation and sympathy for human convenience are called for, there is no

---

[65] According to the U.S. Department of Housing and Urban Development, there are as many as 3.5 million people experience homelessness in a given year.

[66] By 2005, the U.S. government provided $120 billion in subsidies for affordable housing, representing nearly 80 percent of all federal housing assistance. However, at a rate of 1.2 million households (receiving those subsidies today), even at 1960s rates, the "ideal" amount is 2.4 trillion (120 billion x 20, 000), whereas only 120 billion has been provided. "Changing Priorities The Federal Budget and Housing Assistance 1976–2005" (p.17). *The National Low Income Housing Coalition*, October 2004.

forethought and we drift aimlessly; when there is planning, it is abstract and aimed at keeping things under control. For instance, in the last sentence of my previous paragraph, I contrast "$20,000 a unit" with "staying home," but no such equation could occur in urban planning, for the word "home" has ceased to exist; the term is "dwelling unit" or D.U. The D.U. is analyzed to meet certain biological and sociological criteria, and it is also restricted by certain rules, e.g. in public housing one cannot nail a picture on the wall, climb a tree in the landscaping, keep pets, engage in immoral sex, or get a raise in salary. There is a theory, as yet unproved, that planning can dispense with the concept "home"; it is a debased version of LeCorbusier's[67] formula that a house is a machine for living, equal for any tenant and therefore controlled to be interchangeable. But is it the case that people thrive without an own place, unanalyzable because it is the matrix in which other functions occur and is idiosyncratic? Maybe they can, maybe they can't. My point is not that the D.U. is not so good as the shack in a white supremacist county down South; it is better. But that home in a shack plus $1,000[68] a year to improve it is much better even down South, where money talks as loud as elsewhere.

Another term that has vanished from planning vocabulary is "city." Instead there are urban areas. There is no longer an art of city-planning but a science of urbanism, which analyzes and relates the various urban functions, taking into account priorities and allocating available finances. There is no architectonic principle of civic identification or community spirit which the planner shares as a citizen and in terms of which he makes crucial decisions, including uneconomic choices. Such a principle is perhaps unrealistic in a natural culture, economy, and technology; we are citizens of the United States, not of New York City. In planning, the interstate and national highway plan will surely be laid down first and local amenity

---

[67] Charles-Édouard Jeanneret, better known as Le Corbusier (1887–1965) was a Swiss architect, designer, urbanist, writer and painter, famous for being one of the pioneers of what now is called modern architecture. He was a pioneer in studies of modern high design and was dedicated to providing better living conditions for the residents of crowded cities.
[68] Using a Purchasing Power Calculator the relative value of this amount today is $6,720.00. This answer is obtained by multiplying $1000 by the percentage increase in the Consumer Price Index from 1966 to 2010.

or existing situations must conform to it; and Washington's ideas about the type of financing, and administration of housing will surely determine what is built. (Oddly, just in such urban functions as highways and housing, local patriotism and neighborhood feeling suddenly assert themselves and exert a veto, though rarely providing a plan of their own.)

But is it the case that urban areas, rather than cities, are governable? Every municipality deplores the lack of civic pride, for instance in littering and vandalism, but it is a premise of its own planning. Anomie is primarily giving up on the immediate public environment: the children are bitten by rats, so why bother? The river stinks, so why bother? This kind of depression can go as far as tuberculosis,[69] not to speak of mental disease. In my opinion it is particularly impossible for the young to grow up without a community or local patriotism, for the locality is their only real environment. In any case, when the going gets rough, which happens more and more frequently in American cities, poor people retreat into their neighborhoods and cry "It's ours!" or they burn them because they are not citizens in their own place. The middle class, as usual, makes a more rational choice: since the center offers neither home nor city nor an acceptable environment for their children, they leave it, avoiding its jurisdiction, taxes, and responsibilities, but staying near enough to exploit its jobs and services.

It is painfully reminiscent of imperial Rome, the return of the farmland to swamp and the flight of the *optimati*[70] from the city center. The central city is occupied by a stinking mob who can hardly be called citizens, and the periphery by the knights and senators who are no longer interested in being citizens. This is an urban area.

---

[69] In 2007 there were an estimated 13.7 million chronic active cases, and in 2010 8.8 million new cases, and 1.45 million deaths, mostly in developing countries (World Health Organization, 2009). In addition, more people in the developing world contract tuberculosis because their immune systems are more likely to be compromised due to higher rates of AIDS.

[70] They wished to limit the power of the popular assemblies, and to extend the power of the Senate, which was viewed as more dedicated to the interests of the aristocrats who held the reins of power.

3

Moral defects are disastrous in the long run; but American cities are also vulnerable to more immediate dangers, to life and limb. In my own city of New York, during the past year we have been visited by ten critical plagues, some of them temporary emergencies that could recur at any time, some abiding sores that are getting worse. It is interesting to list these and notice the responses of New Yorkers to them.

There was a power failure that for a few hours blacked out everything and brought most activity to a stop. There was a subway and bus strike that for a couple of weeks slowed down everything and disrupted everybody's business. There was a threatened water shortage persisting for four years and which, if the supply had really failed, would probably have made the city unlivable. In these "objective" emergencies, the New Yorkers responded with fine citizenship, good humor, and mutual aid. By and large, they remember the emergencies as better than business as usual. Everybody was in the same boat.

(By contrast, during the long heat wave of last summer—no joke in the asphalt oven of a giant city—there was less enthusiasm. In Chicago it was the occasion for a bad race riot, when a fire hydrant was shut off in a black American neighborhood but, it was said, not in a white neighborhood. In New York it came out that the poor in public housing could not use air-conditioners because of inadequate wiring. Evidently, everybody was not in the same boat.)

The rivers and bays are polluted and often stink; in a huge city with no open space and few facilities for recreation, this is a calamity. The air is bad but not critical, so I will not include it. The congestion is critical. Traffic often hardly moves, and new highways will only make the situation worse; there is no solution but to ban private cars, but no politician has the nerve to do it. As for human crowding, it is hard to know at what density people can no longer adapt, but there must be a point at which there are too many signals and the circuits become clogged, and where people do not have enough social space to feel self-possessed. In some areas, in my opinion, we have passed that point. In Harlem, there are 67,000[71] to the square mile; people live two and three to a room; and the average child of 12 will not have been half a mile from home.

Toward these abiding ills, the attitude of New Yorkers is characteristically confused. They overwhelmingly, and surprisingly, vote a billion dollars to clean up the pollution; they cooperate without grumbling with every gimmick to speed up traffic (though taxi-drivers tell me most of them are a lot of nonsense); they are willing to pay bigger bills than anywhere else for public housing and schools. As people they are decent. But they are entirely lacking in determination to prevent the causes and to solve the conditions; they do not believe that anything will be done, and they accept this state of things. As citizens they are washouts.

Finally, there are the plagues that indicate breakdown, psychopathology and sociopathology. There are estimated 70,000 dope-addicts, with the attendant desperate petty burglary. The juvenile delinquency starts like urban, juvenile delinquency of the past, but it persists into addiction or other social withdrawal because there is less neighborhood support and less economic opportunity. Families have now grown up for several generations dependent on relief, reformatories, public hospitals, and asylums as the normal course of life. A psychiatric survey of midtown Manhattan has shown that 75% have marked neurotic symptoms and 25% need psychiatric treatment, which is of course unavailable.

Given the stress of such actual physical and psychological dangers, we can no longer speak, in urban sociology, merely of urban loneliness, alienation, mechanization, delinquency, class and racial tensions, and so forth. Anomie is one thing; fearing for one's life and sanity is another. On the present scale, urbanization is an unique phenomenon and we must expect new consequences. To put it another way, it becomes increasingly difficult for candid observers to distinguish between populist protest, youth alienation, delinquency, mental disease, civil disobedience, and outright riot. All sometimes

---

[71] As of 2011, this amount has decreased to 55,760. http://www.city-data.com/neighborhood/Harlem-New-York-NY.html (Jan. 2012).

seem to be equally political; at other times, all seem to be merely symptomatic.

4

Inevitably, the cities are in financial straits. (At a recent Senate hearing, Mayor Lindsay of New York explained that to make the city "livable" would require $50 billion[72] more in the next ten years, over and above the normal revenue.) Since they are not ecologically viable, the costs for services, transportation, housing, schooling, welfare, and policing steadily mount with diminishing benefits. Meantime, the blighted central city provides less revenue; the new middle class, as we have seen, pays its taxes in suburban counties; and in the state legislatures the rural counties, which are over-represented because of the drastic shift in population, are stingy about paying for specifically urban needs, which are indeed out of line in cost. Radical liberals believe, of course, that all troubles can be immensely helped if urban areas get much more money from national and state governments, and they set store by the re-apportionment of the state legislatures as ordered by the Supreme Court. In my opinion, if the money is spent for the usual liberal social-engineering, for more freeways, bureaucratic welfare and schooling, bulldozing Urban Renewal, subsidized suburbanization, and police, it will not only fail to solve the problems but will aggravate them, it will increase the anomie, the crowding.

The basic error is to take the present urbanization for granted, both in style and extent, rather than to rethink it: (1) To alleviate anomie, we must, however "inefficient" and hard to administer it may be, avoid the present massification and social engineering; we must experiment with new forms of democracy, so that the urban areas can become cities again and the people citizens. I shall return to this subject in the following lectures. But (2) to relieve the absolute over-crowding that has already occurred or is imminent, nothing else will do but a certain amount of dispersal, which is

---

[72] The relative value of this amount today is about 271 billion. This answer is obtained by the same method as stated earlier in note 66.

unlikely in this generation in the United States. It involves rural reconstruction and the building up of the country towns that are their regional capitals. (I do not mean New Towns, Satellite Towns, or Dormitory Towns.) In Scheme II of *Communitas*,[73] my brother and I have fancifully sketched such a small regional city, on anarcho-syndicalist principles, as a symbiosis of farm and city activities and values. (Incidentally, Scheme II would make a lot of sense in Canada.) But this is Utopian. In this lecture let me rather outline some principles of rural reconstruction for the United States at present, during a period of excessive urbanization.

Liberals, when they think about urbanization, either disregard the country or treat it as an enemy in the legislature. A result of such a policy is to aggravate still another American headache, depressed rural areas. The few quixotic friends of rural reconstruction, on the other hand, like Ralph Borsodi[74] and the people of the Green Revolution, cut loose from urban problems altogether as from a sinking ship. But this is morally unrealistic, since in fact serious people cannot dissociate themselves from the main problems of society; they would regard themselves as deeply useless—just as small farmers do consider themselves. A possible basis of rural reconstruction, however, is for the country to help with urban problems, where it can more cheaply and far more effectively, and thus to become socially important again. (An heroic example is how the Israeli kibbutzim helped with the influx of the hundreds of thousands of Oriental Jews who came destitute and alien.)

Radicals, what I have called the wave of urban populists, the students, black Americans, radical professors, and just irate citizens, are on this subject no better than the liberals. They are busy and inventive about new forms of urban democracy, but they are sure to call the use of the country and rural reconstruction reactionary. Typically, if I suggest to a Harlem leader that some of the children

---

[73] *Communitas: Means of Livelihood and Ways of Life*, with Percival Goodman (Chicago: University of Chicago Press, 1947).

[74] Ralph Borsodi (1886–1977) was an agrarian theorist and practical experimenter interested in ways of living useful for the modern family who desire greater self-reliance. Much of his theory related to living in rural surroundings on a modern homestead.

might do better boarding with a farmer and going to a village school, somewhat like children of the upper middle class, I am told that I am downgrading black Americans by consigning them to the sticks. It is a curious reversal of the narrowness of the agrarian populism of eighty years ago. At that time the farmers lost out by failing to ally themselves with city industrial workers, who were regarded as immoral foreigners and coolie[75] labor. Now farmers are regarded as backward fools, like one's sharecropper father. Although the urban areas are patently unlivable, they have narrowed their inhabitants' experience so that no other choice seems available.

In Canada, a more rational judgment is possible. You have a rural ratio–15-20%, including independent fishermen, lumberers, etc.–that we ought to envy.[76] Your cities, though in need of improvement, are manageable in size. There is still a nodding acquaintance between city and country. I urge you not to proceed down our primrose path, but to keep the ratio you have and, as your technology and population grow, to work out a better urban-rural symbiosis.

5

Traditionally in the United States, farming as a way of life and the maintenance of a high rural ratio have been regarded as the source of all moral virtue and political independence; but by and large public policy has tended to destroy them. The last important attempt to increase small farming was during the Great Depression when subsistence farms were subsidized as a social stabilizer, preferable to shanties in the park and breadlines. The program lapsed with the war-production prosperity that we still enjoy, and for twenty years, as we have seen, public policy has conspired to liquidate rural life completely. There were no Jeffersonian protests when President Johnson declared two years ago that it is his intention to get two-million more families off the land. (Lo and behold, this year LBJ has

---

[75] Historically, a **coolie** was a manual labourer or slave from Asia, particularly China, the Indian subcontinent, and the Philippines during the 19th century and early 20th century.

[76] This figure is about 20 percent today, or 6,262,154 (Statistic Canada, 2006). The American figure is half, or ten percent. See note 60.

made a speech for massive migration to the land!) Nevertheless, in the present emergency of excessive urbanization, let me offer five ideas for rural reconstruction:

(1) At once re-assign to the country urban services that can be better performed there. Especially to depopulating areas, to preserve what there is. And do not do this by setting up new urban-run institutions in the country, but using local families, facilities and institutions, administered by the new underemployed county agents, Farmers Union, 4-H Clubs,[77] and town governments. Consider a few examples:

For a slum child who has never been half a mile from home, a couple of years boarding with a farm family and attending a country school is what anthropologists call a culture-shock, opening wide the mind. The cost per child in a New York grade school is $850[78] a year. Let us divide this sum equally between farmer and local school. Then, the farmer gets $30 a week for three boarders (whom he must merely feed well and not beat), and add on some of the children's welfare money, leaving some for the mothers in the city. With a dozen children, $5,000, the under-used school can buy a new teacher or splendid new equipment. Add on the school lunch subsidy.

In New York City or Chicago, $2,500 a year of welfare money buys a family destitution and undernourishment. In beautiful depopulating areas of Vermont, Maine, or upper New York State, or southern Iowa and northern Wisconsin, it is sufficient for a decent life and even owning a house and land. (Indeed, if we had a reasonable world, the same sum would make a family quite well-to-do in parts of Mexico, Greece, or even Ireland.)

The same reasoning applies to the aged. Given the chance, many old people would certainly choose to while away the years in a small village or on a farm, where they would be more part of life and

---

[77] **4-H** in the United States is a youth organization administered by United States Department of Agriculture. The name represents four personal development areas of focus for the organization: head, heart, hands, and health. The goal of 4-H is to develop citizenship, leadership, responsibility and life skills of youth through experiential learning programs and a positive youth development approach.

[78] This amount today would be about 10 000 dollars. Wall Street Journal, May 25, 2011.

might be useful, instead of in an institution with occupational therapy.

Vacations are an expensive function in which the city uses the country and the country the city. In simpler times, when the rural ratio was high, people exchanged visits with their country cousins or sent the children "to the farm." At present, vacations from the city are largely spent at commercial resorts that tend rather to destroy the country communities than to support them. There are many ways to revive the substance of the older custom, and it is imperative to do so in order to have some social space and escape, which, needless to say, the urbanized resorts do not provide.

Here is a more touchy example: the great majority of inmates in our vast public mental institutions are harmless themselves but in danger on the city streets. Many, perhaps most, rot away without treatment. A certain number would be better off—and there would be more remissions—if they roamed remote villages and the countryside as the local eccentrics or loonies, and if they lived in small nursing homes or with farm families paid well to fetch them home. (I understand that this system worked pretty well in Holland.)

(2) Most proposals like these, however, require changes in jurisdiction and administrative purpose. A metropolitan school board will not give up a slum child, though the cost is the same and the classrooms are crowded. No municipality will pay welfare money to a non-resident to spend elsewhere. (I do not know the attitude in this respect of frantically overworked mental hospitals, which do try to get the patients out.) Besides, often in the American federal system, one cannot cross state lines: a New York child would not get state education aid in Vermont.

So, in conditions of excessive urbanization, let us define a "region" symbiotically rather than economically or technologically. It is the urban area and the surrounding country with a contrasting way of life and different conditions that can therefore help solve urban human problems. This classical conception of the capital and its province is the opposite of usual planning. In terms of transportation and business, planners regard the continuous conurbation from north of Boston to Washington as one region and ask for authority to override state and municipal boundaries; for tax purposes, New

York would like authority to treat the suburban counties as part of the New York region. These things are, I think, necessary; but their effect must certainly be to increase the monstrous conurbation and make it even more homogeneous. If I regard Vermont, northern New Hampshire and New York, and central Pennsylvania as part of the urban area, however, the purpose of the regional authority is precisely to prevent conurbation and strengthen locality, to make the depopulating areas socially important by their very difference.

(3) The chief use of small farming, at present, cannot be for cash but for its independence, simplicity, and abundance of subsistence; and to make the countryside beautiful. Rural reconstruction must mainly depend on other sources of income, providing urban social services and, as is common, part-time factory work. Nevertheless, we ought carefully to re-examine the economics of agriculture, the real costs and the quality of the product. With some crops, certainly with specialty and gourmet foods, the system of intensive cultivation and hothouses serving farmers' markets in the city and contracting with restaurants and hotels, is quite efficient; it omits processing and packaging, cuts down on the cost of transportation, and is indispensable for quality. The development of technology in agriculture has no doubt been as with technology in general, largely determined by economic policy and administration. If there were a premium on small intensive cultivation, as in Holland, technology would develop to make it the "most efficient."

In our big cities, suburban development has irrevocably displaced nearby truck gardening. But perhaps in the next surrounding ring, now often devastated, small farming can revive even for cash.

(4) National TV, movies, news services, etc., have offset provincial narrowness and rural idiocy, but they have also had a more serious effect of brainwashing than in, at least, the big cities which have more intellectual resistance. Country culture has quite vanished. Typical are the county papers which now contain absolutely nothing but conventional gossip notes and ads.

Yet every region has seventeen TV channels available, of which only three or four are used by the national networks. (I think the Americans would be wise to have also a public national channel like

CBC.)[79] Small broadcasting stations would be cheap to run if local people would provide the programs. That is, there is an available community voice if there were anything to say. The same holds for little theaters and local newspapers. I have suggested elsewhere that such enterprises, and small design offices and laboratories, could provide ideal apprenticeships for bright high school and college youth who are not academic and who now waste their time and the public money in formal schools. These could be adolescents either from the country or the city. (In New York, it costs up to $1,400 a year to keep an adolescent in a blackboard jungle.)[80] Perhaps if communities got used to being participants and creators rather than spectators and consumers of canned information, entertainment, and design, they might recall what they are about.

All such cultural and planning activities, including the sociology of the urban services, ought to be the concern of the land grant college. At present in the United States we have pathetically perverted this beautiful institution. The land-grant college, for "mechanics and agriculture," was subsidized to provide cultural leadership for its region, just as the academic university was supposed to be international and to teach humanities and humane professions. But now our land-grant and other regional colleges have lost their community function and become imitations of the academic schools, usually routine and inadequate, while the academic universities have alarmingly been corrupted to the interests of the nation and the national corporations. Naturally, the more its best young are trained to be personnel of the urban system, the more the country is depleted of brains and spirit.

(5) The fruition of rural reconstruction would consist of two things: a strong co-operative movement and a town-meeting democracy[81] that makes sense, in its own terms, on big regional and national issues. A century ago Tocqueville spoke with admiration of how the Americans formed voluntary associations to run society; they were engaged citizens. This would seem to be the natural tendency of independent spirits conscious of themselves as socially

---

[79] PBS is similar, but unlike the CBC, PBS is not publically funded.
[80] Or around 10 000 dollars in today's currency. See Note 76.
[81] This is what Goodman means by "Jeffersonian."

important; they can morally afford to pool their resources for their own purposes. At present it is dismaying to see individual farmers, almost on the margin, each buying expensive machinery to use a few days a year, and all totally unable to co-operate in processing or distribution. They are remarkably skillful men in a dozen crafts and sciences, but they are like children. They feel that they do not count for anything. And unable to co-operate with one another, they cannot compete and they do not count for anything. Correspondingly, their political opinions, which used to be stubbornly sensible though narrow, are frightened, and parrot the national rhetoric as if they never engaged in dialogue and had no stake of their own.

6

To sum up, in the United States the excessive urbanization certainly cannot be thinned out in this generation and we are certainly in for more trouble. In some urban functions, perhaps, like schooling, housing, and the care of mental disease, thinning out by even a few percent would be useful; and the country could help in this and regain some importance in the big society, which is urban. Nevertheless, the chief advantage of rural reconstruction is for its own sake, as an alternative way of life. It could develop a real countervailing power because it is relatively independent; it is not like the orthodox pluralism of the sociologists that consists of differences that make no difference because the groups depend on one another so tightly that they form a consensus willy-nilly.

The Scandinavian countries are a good model for us. By public policy over a century and a half, they have maintained a high rural ratio; for a century they have supported a strong co-operative movement; and they have devised a remarkably various and thoughtful system of education. These things are not unrelated, and they have paid off in the most decent advanced society that there is, with a countervailing mixed economy, a responsible bureaucracy, and vigilant citizens.

THE PSYCHOLOGY OF BEING HELPLESS   V

Americans believe that the great background conditions of modern life are beyond our power to influence. The abuse of technology is autonomous and cannot be checked. The galloping urbanization is going to gallop on. Our over-centralized administration, both of things and men, is impossibly cumbersome and costly, but we cannot cut it down to size. These are inevitable tendencies of history. More dramatic inevitabilities, in the popular belief, are the explosions, the scientific explosion and the population explosion. And there are more literal explosions, the dynamite accumulating in the slums of a thousand cities and the accumulating stockpiles of nuclear bombs in nations great and small. Our psychology, in brief, is that history is out of control. It is no longer something that we make but something that happens to us. Politics is not prudent steering in difficult terrain, but it is—and this is the subject of current political science—how to get power and keep power, even though the sphere of effective power is extremely limited and it makes little difference who is in power. The psychology of historical powerlessness is evident in the reporting and the reading of newspapers: there is little analysis of how events are building up, but we read—with excitement, spite, or fatalism, depending on our characters—the headlines of crises for which we are unprepared. Statesmen cope with emergencies, and the climate of emergency is chronic.

I have been trying to show that some of these historical conditions are not inevitable at all but are the working out of willful policies that aggrandize certain interests and exclude others, that subsidize certain styles and prohibit others. But of course, *historically,* if almost everybody believes the conditions are inevitable, including the policy makers who produce them, then they are inevitable. For to cope with emergencies does not mean, then, to support alternative conditions, but further to support and institutionalize the same conditions. Thus, if there are too many cars, we build new highways; if administration is too cumbersome, we build in new levels of administration; if there is a nuclear threat, we develop anti-missile missiles; if there is urban crowding and anomie, we step up urban renewal and social work; if there are ecological disasters because of imprudent use of technology, we subsidize Research and Development by the same scientific corporations working for the same ecologically irrelevant motives; if there is youth alienation, we extend and intensify schooling; if the nation-state is outmoded as a political form, we make ourselves into a mightier nation-state.

In this self-proving round, the otherwise innocent style of input-output economics, games-theory strategy,[82] and computerized social science becomes a trap. For the style dumbly accepts the self-proving program and cannot compute what is not mentioned. Then the solutions that emerge ride even more roughshod over what has been left out. Indeed, at least in the social sciences, the more variables one can technically compute, the less likely it is that there will be prior thinking about their import, rather than interpretation of their combination. Our classic example—assuming that there will

---

[82] Game theory is a mathematical method for analyzing calculated circumstances, such as in games, where a person's success is based upon the choices of others. More formally, it is the study of mathematical models of conflict and cooperation between intelligent rational decision-makers.

be a future period to which we provide classic examples—is Herman Kahn[83] on Thermonuclear War.

In this lecture, therefore, I will no longer talk about the error of believing that our evils are necessary, but stick to the more interesting historical fact of that belief. What is the psychology of feeling that one is powerless to alter basic conditions? What is it as a way of being in the world? Let me list half a dozen kinds of responses to being in a chronic emergency; unfortunately, in America they are exhibited in rather pure form. I say unfortunately, because a pure response to a chronic emergency is a neurotic one; healthy human beings are more experimental or at least muddling. Instead of politics, we now have to talk psychotherapy.

2

By definition, governors cannot forfeit the symbol that everything is under control, though they may not think so. During President Kennedy's administration, Arthur Schlesinger[84] expressed the problem poignantly by saying, "One simply *must* govern." The theme of that administration was to be "pragmatic"; but by this they did not mean a philosophical pragmatism, going toward an end in view from where one in fact is and with the means one has; they meant turning busily to each crisis as it arose, so that it was clear that one was not inactive. The criticism of Eisenhower's administration was that it was stagnant. The new slogan was "get America moving."

This was rather pathetic; but as the crises have become deeper, the response of the present administration is not pathetic but,

---

[83] Herman Kahn (1922–1983) was a founder of the Hudson Institute think tank and originally came to prominence as a military strategist and systems theorist while employed at RAND Corporation, USA. His theories contributed to the development of the nuclear strategy of the United States.

[84] Arthur Schlesinger, Jr. (1917 - 2007) was an American historian and social critic whose work explored the American liberalism of political leaders including Franklin D. Roosevelt, John F. Kennedy, and Robert F. Kennedy. A Pulitzer Prize winner, Schlesinger served as special assistant and "court historian" to President Kennedy from 1961 to 1963.

frankly, delusional and dangerous. It is to *will* to be in control, without adjusting to the realities. They seem to imagine that they will in fact buy up every economy, police the world, social-engineer the cities, school the young. In this fantasy they employ a rhetoric of astonishing dissociation between idea and reality, far beyond customary campaign oratory. For example, they proclaim that they are depolluting streams, but they allot no money; forty "demonstration cities" are to be made livable and show the way, but the total sum available is $1.5 billion (we saw that Mayor Lindsay asked for 50 billions for New York alone); the depressed area of Appalachia has been reclaimed, but the method is an old highway bill under another name; poor people will run their own programs, but any administrator is fired if he tries to let them; they are suing for peace, but they dispatch more troops and bombers. This seems to be just lying but, to my ear, it is nearer to magic thinking. The magic buoys up the self-image; the activity is either nothing at all or brute force to make the problem vanish.

In between the ideality and the brutality there occurs a lot of obsessional warding off of confusion by methodical calculations that solve problems in the abstract, in high modern style. A precise decimal is set beyond which the economy will be inflationary, but nobody pays any mind to it. We know at what average annual income how many peoples cause what percentage of disturbances. A precise kill-ratio is established beyond which the Viet Cong[85] will fold up, but they don't. Polls are consulted for the consensus, like the liver of sheep, without noticing signs of unrest and even though the administration keeps committing itself to an irreversible course that allows for no choice. And they are everlastingly righteous.

---

[85] The Viet Cong or National Liberation Front was a political organization and army in South Vietnam and Cambodia that fought the United States and South Vietnamese governments during the Vietnam War (1959–1975).

In more insane moments, however, they manufacture history out of the whole cloth, so there is no way of checking up at all. They create incidents in order to exact reprisals; they invent (and legislate about) agitators for demonstrations and riots that are spontaneous; they project bogey-men in order to arm to the teeth. Some of this, to be sure, is cynical, but that does not make it less mad; for, clever at it or not, they still avoid the glaring realities of world poverty, American isolation, mounting urban costs, mounting anomie, and so forth. I do not think the slogan, "The Great Society,"[86] is cynical; it is delusional.

Perhaps the epitome of will operating in panic—like a case from a textbook in abnormal psychology—has been the government's handling of the assassination of John Kennedy. The Warren Commission[87] attempted to "close" the case, to make it not exist in the public mind. Thus it hastily drew firm conclusions from dubious evidence, disregarded counter-evidence, defied physical probabilities, and even may have accepted manufactured evidence. For a temporary lull it has run the risk of total collapse of public trust that may end up in a Dreyfus case.

3

Common people, who do not have to govern, can let themselves feel powerless and resign themselves. They respond with the familiar combination of not caring and, as a substitute, identifying with those whom they fancy to be powerful. This occurs differently, however, among the poor and the middle class.

The poor simply stop trying, become dependent, drop out of school, drop out of sight, become addicts, become lawless. It seems

[86] See note 27.
[87] The Warren Commission took its unofficial name from its chairman, Chief Justice Earl Warren. It was established by Lyndon B. Johnson to investigate the assassination of President John F. Kennedy. It concluded that Lee Harvey Oswald acted alone in the killing of Kennedy, and that Jack Ruby acted alone in the murder of Oswald.

to be a matter of temperature or a small incident whether or not they riot. As I have said before, in anomic circumstances it is hard to tell when riot or other lawlessness is a political act toward a new set-up and when it is a social pathology. Being powerless as citizens, poor people have little meaningful structure in which to express, or know, what they are after. The concrete objects of their anger make no political sense: they are angry at themselves or their own neighborhoods, at white people passing by, at Jewish landlords and shopkeepers. More symbolic scapegoats like either "the capitalist system" or "communism" do not evoke much interest. One has to feel part of a system to share its bogey-men or have a counter-ideology, and by and large the present-day poor are not so much exploited as excluded.

But to fill the void, they admire, and identify with, what is strong and successful, even if–perhaps especially if– it is strong and successful at their own expense. Poor Spanish youth are enthusiastic about our mighty bombs and bombers, though of course they have no interest in the foreign policy that uses them. (If anything, poor people tend to be for de-escalation and peace rather than war.) Readers of the *Daily News* are excited by the dramatic confrontation of statesmen wagging fingers at each other. Blacks in Harlem admire the Cadillacs of their own corrupt politicians and racketeers. Currently there is excitement about the words "Black Power," but the confusion about the meaning is telling: in the South, where there is little Negro[88] anomie, Black Power has considerable political meaning; in the northern cities it is a frantic abstraction. Similarly, the contrary word "Integration" makes economic and pedagogic sense if interpreted by people who have some feeling of freedom and power, but if interpreted by resentment and hopelessness it turns

---

[88] See note 15.

into a fight for petty victories or spite, which are not political propositions, though they may be good for the soul.

The anomie of middle-class people, on the other hand, appears rather as their privatism; they retreat to their families and consumer goods where they still have some power and choice. It is always necessary to explain to non-Americans that middle-class Americans are not so foolish and piggish about their Standard of Living as it seems; it is that the Standard of Living has to provide all the achievement and value that are open to them. But it is a strange thing for a society to be proud of its Standard of Living, rather than taking it for granted as a background for worthwhile action.

Privacy is purchased at a terrible price of anxiety, excluding, and pettiness, the need to delete anything different from oneself and to protect things that are not worth protecting. Nor can they be protected; few of the suburban homes down the road, that look so trim, do not have cases of alcoholism, insanity, youngsters on drugs, or in jail for good or bad reasons, ulcers, and so forth. In my opinion, middle-class squeamishness and anxiety, a kind of obsessional neurosis, are a much more important cause of segregation than classical race-prejudice which is a kind of paranoia that shows up most among failing classes, bankrupt small property owners, and proletarians under competitive pressure. The squeamishness is worse, for it takes people out of humanity, whereas prejudice is at least passionate. Squeamishness finally undercuts even the fairness and decency that we expect from the middle class.

The identification with power of the powerless middle class is also characteristic. They do not identify with brutality, big men, or wealth, but with the efficient system itself, which is what renders *them* powerless. And here again we can see the sharp polarity between those who are not politically resigned and those who are. Take the different effects of what is called education. On the one hand, the universities, excellent students and distinguished professors, are the nucleus of opposition to our war policy. On the other hand, in general polls there is always a dismaying correlation between years of schooling and the "hard line" of bombing China during the Korean War or bombing Hanoi now. But this is not because the educated middle class is rabidly anti-communist, and certainly it is not ferocious; rather, it is precisely because it is rational, it approves the technically efficient solution that does not notice flesh and blood suffering. In this style the middle class feels it has status, though no more power than anybody else. No doubt these middle-class people are influenced by the magazines they read,[89] which explain what *is* efficient; but they are influenced because they are "thinking" types, for whom reality is what they read.

The bathos of the irresponsible middle class is the nightly TV newscast on our national networks. This combines commercials for the High Standard of Living, scenes of war and riot, and judicious pro-and-con commentary on what it all means. The scenes arouse feeling, the commentary provokes thought, the commercials lead to action. It is a total experience.

4

Let me illustrate the anomic psychology with another example, for it has come to be accepted as the normal state of feeling rather than as pathological. (I apologize to the Canadian audience for choosing my example again from the Vietnam War. But my country is bombing and burning those people, and my friends and I are unable to prevent it.)

During the hearings on Vietnam before the Senate Foreign Relations Committee,[90] Senator Dodd of Connecticut was asked

---

[89] We could of course add the time spent surfing the Internet.

[90] The Senate Foreign Relations Committee, chaired by Democratic Senator J. William Fulbright of Arkansas, began to hear testimony on the War in Vietnam in 1966 and continued until 1972. The hearings included testimony and debate from several members of Congress, as well as from representatives of interested pro-war and anti-war organizations.

what he thought of the sharp criticism of the government. "It is the price we pay," he said, "for living in a free country." This answer was routine and nobody questioned it. Yet what an astonishing evaluation of the democratic process it is, that free discussion is a weakness we must put up with in order to avoid the evils of another system! To Milton, Spinoza, or Jefferson free discussion was the strength of a society. Their theory was that truth had power, often weak at first but steady and cumulative, and in free debate the right course would emerge and prevail. Nor was there any other method to arrive at truth, since there was no other authority to pronounce it than all the people. Thus, to arrive at wise policy, it was essential for everybody to say his say, and the more disparate the views and searching the criticism the better.

Instead, Senator Dodd seems to have the following epistemology of democracy: We elect an administration and it, through the intelligence service, secret diplomacy, briefings by the Department of Defense and other agencies, comes into inside information that enables it alone to understand the situation. In principle we can repudiate its decisions at the next election, but usually they have led to commitments and actions that are hard to repudiate. Implicit is that there is a permanent group of selfless and wise public servants, experts and impartial reporters, who understand the technology, strategy, and diplomacy that we cannot understand, and therefore we must perforce do what they advise. To be sure, they continually make bad predictions and, on the evidence, they are not selfish but partial or at least narrow in their commercial interests and political outlook. Yet this does not alter the picture, for if the President goes along with them, outside criticism is irrelevant anyway and no doubt misses the point, which, it happens, cannot be disclosed for reasons of national security. And surely irrelevant discussion is harmful because it is divisive. But it is the price we pay for living in a free country.

What can be the attraction of such a diluted faith in democracy? It is what is appropriate in a chronic low-grade emergency. In an emergency it is rational, and indeed natural, to concentrate temporary power in a small center, as the ancient Romans appointed dictators, to decide and act, and for the rest of us to support the *faits accomplis* for better or worse. But since we face a low-grade emergency—nobody is about to invade San Francisco—we like to go on as usual, including sounding off and criticizing, so long as it does not effect policy.

Unfortunately, this psychology keeps the low-grade emergency chronic. There is no way to get back to normal, no check on *faits accomplis,* no accountability of the decision-makers till so much damage has been done that there is a public revulsion (as after a few years of Korea[91]), or, as seems inevitable, one day a catastrophe. Worst of all there is no way for a philosophic view to emerge that might become effectual. Who would present such a view? In the classical theory of democracy, the electorate is educated by the clashing debate and the best men come forward and gain a following. But in Senator Dodd's free country, acute men are likely to fall silent, for what is the use of talk that is irrelevant and divisive?

The discussion in the Foreign Relations Committee, excellent as it was, was itself typical of a timid democracy. Not a single Senator was able to insist on basic realities that could put the Vietnam War in a philosophic light and perhaps work out of its dilemmas. (Since then, Senator Fulbright has become more outspoken.) In this context, here are some of the basic realities: In a period of world-wide communications and spread of technology, and therefore of

---

[91] The Korean War (1950–1953) was a war between the (Southern) Republic of Korea (supported by the United Nations) and the (Northern) Democratic People's Republic of Korea (supported by the People's Republic of China, with military and material aid from the Soviet Union).

"rising aspirations," nevertheless a majority of mankind is fast becoming poorer. For our own country, is it really in our national interest to come on as a Great Power, touchy about saving face and telling other peoples how to act or else? In the era of One World and the atom bomb, is there not something baroque in the sovereignty of nation states and legalisms about who aggressed on whom?

It will be objected that such anti-national issues can hardly be raised by Senators, even in a free debate. But the same limitation exists outside of government. In the scores of pretentious TV debates and panel discussions on Vietnam during the past two years, I doubt that there have been half a dozen—and these not on national networks—in which a speaker was invited who might conceivably go outside the official parameters and raise the real questions. Almost always the extreme opposition is himself a proponent of power politics, like Hans Morgenthau. (It usually *is* Hans Morgenthau.) Why not A. J. Muste, for instance?[92] Naturally the big networks would say that there is no use in presenting quixotic opinions that are irrelevant. (The word "quixotic" was used by General Sarnoff[93] of the National Broadcasting Company in his successful bid to Congress to deny to third party candidates equal free time.) By this response, the broadcasters guarantee that the opinions will remain irrelevant, until history, "out of control," makes them relevant because they were true.

5

This brings me back to my subject, how people are in the world when history is "out of control." So far I have noticed those who

---

[92] Hans Joachim Morgenthau (1904–1980) was one of the leading twentieth-century figures in the study of international politics. He made landmark contributions to international-relations theory and the study of international law. The Reverend Abraham Johannes "A.J." Muste (1885-1967) was a Dutch-born American clergyman and political activist. Muste is best remembered for his work in the labor movement, pacifist movement, and the US civil rights movement.

[93] David Sarnoff (1891–1971) was an American businessman and pioneer of American commercial radio and television. He founded the National Broadcasting Company. Named a Reserve Brigadier General of the Signal Corps in 1945, Sarnoff thereafter was widely known as "The General."

unhistorically will to be in control and those who accept their powerlessness and withdraw. But there is another possibility, apocalypse, not only to accept being powerless but to expect, or perhaps wish and hasten, the inevitable historical explosion. Again there are two variants, for it is usually a different psychology, entailing different behavior, to expect a catastrophe and beat around for what to do for oneself, or to wish for the catastrophe and identify with it.

To expect disaster and desert the sinking ship is not a political act, but it is often a profoundly creative one, both personally and socially. To do it, one must have vitality of one's own that is not entirely structured and warped by the suicidal system. Going it alone may allow for new development. For instance, when the youth of the Beat movement cut loose from the organized system, opted for voluntary poverty, and invented a morals and culture out of their own guts and some confused literary memories, they exerted a big, and on the whole good, influence. Also, the disposition of the powers-that-be to treat gross realities as irrelevant has driven many intellectual and spirited persons into deviant paths just to make sense of their own experience; thus, at present, perhaps most of the best artists and writers in America are unusually far out of line, even for creative people. They hardly seem to share the common culture, yet they are what culture we have. (According to himself, Dr. Timothy Leary,[94] the psychodelics man, espouses the extreme of this philosophy, "Turn on, tune in, and drop out"; but I doubt that relying on chemicals is really a way of dropping out of our drug-ridden and technological society.)

---

[94] Timothy Francis Leary (1920–1996) was an American psychologist and writer, known for his advocacy of psychedelic drugs. During a time when drugs like LSD and psilocybin were legal, Leary conducted experiments at Harvard University under the Harvard Psilocybin Project, resulting in the Concord Prison Experiment and the Marsh Chapel Experiment. Both studies produced useful data, but Leary and his associate Richard Alpert were fired from the university.

We must remember that with the atom bombs there is a literal meaning to deserting the ship. This factor is always present in the background of the young. For instance, during the Cuban missile crisis I kept getting phone calls from college students asking if they should at once fly to New Zealand. I tried to calm their anxiety by opining that the crisis was only diplomatic maneuvering, but I now think that I was wrong, for eyewitnesses of behavior in Washington at the time tell me that there *was* a danger of nuclear war.

More generally, the psychology of apocalypse and the decision to go it alone are characteristic of waves of populism such as we are now surprisingly witnessing in the United States. The rhetoric of the agrarian populism of the Eighties and Nineties was vividly apocalyptic, and that movement brought forth remarkable feats of co-operation and social invention. The current urban and student populism, as I have pointed out in these lectures, has begun to produce its own para-institutional enterprises, some of which are viable.

The practice of civil disobedience also must often be interpreted in terms of the psychology of apocalypse, but even sympathetic legal analysts of civil disobedience fail to take this into account. It is one thing to disobey a law because the authorities are in moral error on some point, in order to force a test case and to rally opposition and change the law. It is another thing to disobey authorities who are the Whore of Babylon and the Devil's thrones and dominions. In such a case the conscientious attitude may be not respect but disregard and disgust, and it may be more moral for God's creatures to go underground rather than to confront, especially if their theology does not include an article on paradise for martyrs. As a citizen of the uncorrupted polity in exile, it might be one's civil duty to be apparently lawless. There is a fairly clear-cut distinction between civil disobedience in a legitimate order and revolution that may or may not prove its own legitimacy; but the politics and morality of apocalypse fall in between and are ambiguous.

6

Quite different, finally, is the psychology of those who unconsciously or consciously wish for catastrophe and work to bring it about. (Of course, for the best youth to desert the sinking ship also brings about disaster, by default.) The wish for a blow-up occurs in people who are so enmeshed in a frustrating system that they have no vitality apart from it; and their vitality in it is explosive rage.

Very poor people, who have "the culture of poverty," as Oscar Lewis[95] calls it, are rarely so psychologically committed to a dominant social system that they need its total destruction. They have dreams of heaven but not of hellfire. A few exemplary burnings and beheadings mollify their vengeance. Their intellectual leaders, however, who are verbal and willy-nilly psychologically enmeshed in the hated system, might be more apocalyptic. For instance, Malcolm X once told me–it was before his last period which was more rational and political–that he would welcome the atom bombing of New York to vindicate Allah, even though it destroyed his own community. James Baldwin[96] is full of hellfire, but I have never heard much of it in popular religion.

On the whole, at present in the United States the psychology of explosive apocalypse is not to be found among rioting black Americans crying "Bum, baby, bum," nor among utopian beatniks on hallucinogens; it is to be found among people who believe in the

---

[95] Oscar Lewis (1914–1970) was an American anthropologist who is best known for his vivid depictions of the lives of slum dwellers and for postulating that there was a cross-generational culture of poverty among poor people that transcended national boundaries.

[96] James Arthur Baldwin (1924–1987) was a Black American novelist, essayist, playwright, poet, and social critic. He is best known for his novel, *Go Tell It on the Mountain*, and the role he played in the Harlem Renaissance.

system but cannot tolerate the anxiety of its not working out for them. Unfortunately, it is a pretty empty system and anxiety is widespread.

Most obviously there is a large group of people who have been demoted or are threatened with demotion, business-men and small property owners who feel they have been pushed around; victims of inflation; displaced farmers; dissatisfied ex-soldiers; proletarians who have become petty bourgeois but are now threatened by automation or by blacks invading their neighborhoods. Consciously these people do not want a blow-up but power to restore the good old days; but when they keep losing out, they manifest an astounding violence and vigilant- ism and could become the usual mass base for fascism. In foreign policy, where immigration has freer rein, they are for pre-emptive first strikes, bombing China, and so forth. I do not think this group is dangerous in itself—I do not think there is an important Radical Right in the United States—but it is a sounding board to propagate catastrophic ideas to more important groups.

My guess is that, under our bad urban conditions, a more dangerous group is the uncountable number of the mentally ill and psychopathic hoodlums from all kinds of backgrounds. Given the rate of mental disease and the arming and training in violence of hundreds of thousands of young men, there is sure to be an increase of berserk acts that might sometimes amount to a reign of terror, and could create a climate for political enormities. Not to speak of organized Storm Trooping.

The most dangerous group of all, however, is the established but anomic middle class that I described previously. Exclusive, conformist, squeamish, and methodical, it is terribly vulnerable to anxiety. When none of its rational solutions work out, at home or abroad, its patience will wear thin, and then it could coldly support a policy of doom, just to have the problems over with, the way a man counts to three and blows his brains out. But this cold conscious acceptance of a "rational solution" would not be possible if unconsciously there were not a lust for destruction of the constraining system, as sober citizens excitedly watch a house burn down.

The conditions of middle-class life are exquisitely calculated to increase tension and heighten anxiety. It is not so much that the pace is fast—often it consists of waiting around and is slow and boring—but that it is somebody else's pace or schedule. One is continually interrupted. And the tension cannot be normally discharged by decisive action and doing things one's own way. There is competitive pressure to act a role, yet paradoxically one is rarely allowed to do one's best or use one's best judgment. Proofs of success or failure are not tangibly given in the task, but always in some superior's judgment. Spontaneity and instinct are likely to be gravely penalized, yet one is supposed to be creative and sexual on demand. All this is what Freud called civilization and its discontents. Wilhelm Reich[97] showed that this kind of anxiety led to dreams of destruction, self-destruction, and explosion, in order to release tension, feel something, and feel free.

A chronic low-grade emergency is not psychologically static. It builds up to and invites a critical emergency.

But just as we are able to overlook glaring economic and ecological realities, so in our social engineering and system of education glaring psychological realities like anomie and anxiety are regarded almost as if they did not exist.

The psychological climate explains, I think, the peculiar attitude of the Americans toward the escalation of the Vietnam War. (At the

---

[97] Wilhelm Reich (1897–1957) was an Austrian-American psychiatrist and psychoanalyst, known as one of the most radical figures in the history of psychiatry. He was the author of several notable books, including *The Mass Psychology of Fascism* and *Character Analysis*, both published in 1933. Reich worked with Sigmund Freud in the 1920s.

time I am writing this, more bombs are being rained on that little country than on Germany at the peak of World War II, and there is talk of sending half a million men.) The government's statements of purpose are inconsistent week by week and are belied by its actions. Its predictions are ludicrously falsified by what happens. Field commanders lie and are contradicted by the next day's news. Yet a good majority continues to acquiesce with a paralyzed fascination. This paralysis is not indifference, for finally people talk about nothing else—as I in these lectures. One has the impression that it is an exciting attraction of a policy that it is doomed.

I have been giving you a gloomy picture of my country. Our policies range from dishonest to delusional. Our system of interlocking institutions finally mechanically goes its own way and runs over human beings. Our people have become stupid and uncitizenly and are lusting for an explosion.

Nevertheless, let me praise us for a moment. We are headed for trouble but we have moral strengths. We have a healthy good humor, that is neither cynical nor resigned. We are seasoned—we got there first—in the high technology, high standard of living, and other conditions of modern times. I think we have fewer illusions about them than other advanced peoples; we are not so foolish and piggish about them as we seem. Morally, despite what seems, Americans are classless and democratic and cannot think in other terms; and if a case *really* comes to public notice, we will not tolerate an individual's being pushed around—though it certainly takes a lot to get some cases to public notice. We are not cowed by authority. And we are energetic and experimental, though not very intelligent about it.

Perhaps our greatest strength is an historical one. Quixotic as it seems, we have an abiding loyalty to the spirit, and sometimes unfortunately the letter, of the American political system. Unlike in many other countries, our extreme groups—Birchites,[98] students of

---

[98] The John Birch Society is an American political advocacy group that supports anti-communism, limited government, a Constitutional Republic and personal freedom. It has been described as radical right-wing.

the New Left, black Americans who want Black Power–are sincerely loyal to this history and spirit, more loyal indeed than the center is, which is lulled by its self-satisfied belief in social engineering. In a crisis, the great majority will continue to be historically loyal and we will not have fascism or 1984, though we may well have disaster. Thus, to repeat what I said at the beginning of this series of lectures, the question is whether our beautiful libertarian, pluralist, and populist experiment is indeed viable in modern conditions. We *can* make it so, both institutionally and because we have the will; the present trends are not inevitable. However, I am not sure that we will make it so, because of pressure of time and panicking.

2

A few weeks ago I had to give a talk at the dedication of the new law school at Rutgers University. What an exciting period it is for a law student, I said, if the study of law is regarded not as a technique for winning cases but as jurisprudence, the relation of law to justice and politics and the historical changes of law to meet new conditions. In the American tradition, the constitution-makers have been lawyers; and since we have so many new conditions, it is the task of young lawyers to come up with constitutional innovations to keep the American polity alive. Consider some of our unique domestic problems, passing by the whole field of world law, that must be developed almost from scratch. When the media of mass communications require immense capital or, like the broadcasting channels, are scarce and licensed, how to safeguard against *de facto* censorship and the brainwashing that is now evident? When mass compulsory education stretches for longer years, how to give rights to the young so that they are not regimented like conscripts and pro-cessed as things? When nearly half the young adults are obliged to go to college, what are their social, political, and academic rights; what do *Lehrfreiheit* and *Lernfreiheit* now mean? In a hardening mandarin establishment of mutually accrediting universities, state boards, and corporate employers, how to change the licensing of professionals and indeed of ordinary employment, so that competent people are not stymied because they do not have irrelevant diplomas? When corporations have grown to the size of feudal baronies and the lines of communication within them become tenuous, the traditional concepts of responsibility of principal and agent are inadequate; how to protect subordinates as moral beings? what are their rights in the decisions they must execute? As technologies expand and their remote effects cannot be avoided by anybody, how to give citizens an effective voice in the shape of the environment, not to speak of a remedy against abuses? As the technical and staff power of the police and other bureaucracies increases, how to bolster the resources of citizens so that there is a fair contest in court and agency? As the complexity, delays, and distance of ordinary political processes become greater, while often the tension of problems becomes worse, it is inevitable that spirited people will resort to various degrees of protest and civil disobedience; how to encourage this rather than render it destructive by disregarding the need for it or even exacting draconian penalties to stamp it out? Finally, in a national corporate economy most taxes must be channeled through the national government, yet municipal and community functions must still be locally controlled to be humanly relevant; then how to organize jurisdiction and budgeting so that people do not dodge their community responsibilities and yet central authorities do not take over?

Here, I said, are some of the crashingly important legal problems that must be solved in order to make American democracy work.[99] And the behavior of the guild of lawyers is itself a case in point. If they simply accept the present formulations and try to win cases under them, they are avoiding their professional responsibility and giving authority by default to incompetent and unbridled powers, or to the drift of things. The same holds, of course, in other professions: in engineering, when the engineer merely executes a program handed down to him, rather than criticizing the program in terms of its community meaning and remote effects; in education, when a teacher serves as personnel in a school system, rather than contributing to the growing up of the young; in journalism, when a reporter follows an official line or caters to a mass market, rather than reporting the events and trying to tell their meaning. But there is no higher principle or authority (excepting the holy spirit and the nature of things) to which professional authority can be delegated, whether in Washington or the president of a university or the board of directors of a corporation or the electorate. It is only each profession, in touch with its own raw materials, daily practice, the judgment of peers, and its professional tradition that can initiate and decide on professional matters.

3

I chose this list, of course, to invent new rights, duties, and safeguards in our increasingly monolithic system of institutions, to make an effective pluralism. They are nothing but an extension to modern technological and social functions of the checks and

---

[99] See "Citizens United v. Federal Election Commission," 558 U.S. 08-205 (2010), 558 U.S.,130 S. Ct. 876 (January 21, 2010). This was a landmark decision by the United States Supreme Court holding that the First Amendment prohibits government from placing limits on independent spending for political purposes by corporations and unions. Essentially, the American judiciary can now be financed by any corporation.

balances discussions in the *Federalist Papers*[100] that dealt mainly with territorial and commercial functions.

Now we have a school of sociology in the United States, that is the liberal orthodoxy, that holds that democratic rights are effectively secured by our present pluralism of institutions and interest groups, labor, capital, the professions, the universities, religious sects, ethnic groups, sectional interests, government, and the general public. According to this theory, these struggle for advantage and countervail one another, and through them each man can exert influence. Admittedly the institutions and interest groups are centralized and bureaucratized, but this is an advantage; for an individual can compete to rise in his own interest group, and the decision-makers of the various bureaucracies, each backed by massive power, can treat with one another in a rational way according to the rules of the game, for example by collective bargaining, and so avoid unseemly strikes, cut-throat competition, riot, and other disorder. This, in turn, makes possible a general harmony and diminishes everybody's anxiety. It is a sociologist's dream.

I am afraid that there is nothing in this theory. For the genius of our centralized bureaucracies has been, as they interlock, to form a mutually accrediting establishment of decision-makers, with common interests and a common style that nullify the diversity of pluralism. Conflict becomes coalition, harmony becomes consensus, and the social machine runs with no check at all. For instance, our regulatory agencies are wonderfully in agreement with the corporations they regulate. It is almost unheard of for the universities or scientists to say Veto, whether to the pesticides, or the

---

[100] The *Federalist Papers* are a series of 85 articles or essays promoting the ratification of the United States Constitution. These 85 articles were written by Alexander Hamilton, James Madison, John Jay, and were published in two volumes in 1788.

causes of smog, the TV programming, the military strategy, or the moon-shot. (An exception was the fallout from the bomb-testing.) When labor leaders become labor statesmen, somehow the labor movement dies. The farm bloc enters the harmony precisely by getting rid of farming and ceasing to have special interests. Press and broadcasting seem never to have to mount a determined campaign against either official handouts or their advertisers. And as for the classical countervalence of parliamentary democracy, the two- party system, after all the fury of campaigning, it almost never makes any difference which party has won. It seems to me impossible that there should be so much happiness.

But perhaps it is a pre-established harmony. I don't know if there is one power Elite, and I am sure that the conspiratorial System is a paranoia of the radical students; nevertheless, it is said that the President has a file of 25,000 names from which appointments are made, after a computer has brought forth the sub-group that fits the profile for the particular role. These are the good guys who count and who can be counted on to initiate and decide in style. Perhaps these sub-groups are what is left of the Plural Interests, and the file is what we mean by the Establishment. (I don't know if there is actually such a file, but there *is* a police-file of bad guys who use the wrong style.)

There is a metaphysical defect in our pluralism. The competing groups are all after the same values, the same money, the same standard of living and fringe benefits. There can then be fierce competition between groups for a bigger cut in the budget, but there is no moral or constitutional countervalence of interests. Let me put this another way: the bother with the profit system has turned out to be not, as the socialists predicted, that it doesn't work, but that it works splendidly; and so long as a person's activity pays off in the common coin, he doesn't much care about his special vocation, profession, functional independence, way of life, way of being in the community, or corporate responsibility for public good.

In the major decisions that are made by the interlocking decision-makers, the democratic representation of the ordinary person is "virtual" rather than actual, as with the American colonists in the British Parliament. If this is so, there is no pluralism. Interest groups become nothing but means of social engineering, to cushion protest and expedite communication from top down. (In my opinion, by the way, the transmission belt doesn't work. When a group does not have real power, the members simply stop attending meetings. In the New York City school system, it doesn't pay to be an active member of the Parents-Teachers Association.)

4

For a pluralism to work democratically—like a guild socialism, a syndicalist system, or a medieval commune—it must proceed in just the opposite direction than that envisaged by our orthodox sociologists. It must try to increase class consciousness, craft pride, professional autonomy, faculty power in the universities, co-operative enterprise, local patriotism, and rural reconstruction. When members of a group stubbornly stand for something, the association will throw its weight around in the community; when the association insists on its special role in the community that must be accommodated to in its own terms (though not, of course on its terms), the members will be active in the association. What would such a medieval pluralism entail?

In the first place, there would be conflict and not harmony. At present, labor and capital can come to an agreement on wages, hours, and benefits, and pass on the costs; but the situation is much more electric if workers ask, as they should, for a say in the work-process and the quality and utility of the product on which they spend their lives. In an authentic pluralism, a teachers' union will want to determine curriculum, method, and class-size in the public schools; but neither the administrators, the Mayor, nor the parents will agree to this. If the Medical Association comes on as a professional group, it will support rather than oppose community payment of fees, which is good for the health of the poor, but it will also intervene on slum conditions and the narcotic laws. The radio and television people will want some control over how they are edited and programmed. We are currently witnessing the conflicts that arise when ethnic groups are organized in their neighborhoods in an authentically pluralistic fashion.

The peaceful settlement of a dispute by rational means in due process is certainly better than agitated conflict; but it must be my dispute in my terms, and my representative must be my agent; if, as usual, the issue has suffered a sea-change by being taken out of my hands, and I find that once again I have not been taken seriously, the apparent harmony only increases my anxiety rather than diminishes it. If, on the other hand, a conflict is about what we really mean, it will rouse excitement and anger and may cause suffering, but it will diminish anxiety and be safer in the long run.

Next, let us look at the other side of the medal, the specific community responsibility of corporate groups which they now disregard. At present we make a thing of corporations policing themselves—probably wisely, since external regulation does not work anyway—but of course this can help only to prevent abuses, not to guarantee positive performance. Also, if the spirit is lacking, the flesh tends to default. To give a ludicrous example: when our Congress passed a law requiring fair TV coverage on both sides of controversial questions, the broadcasters responded simply by cutting back on controversial programs altogether. (Alas! the bland is also a point of view and sometimes very controversial, but I cannot get the Federal Communications Commission to see it this way.)

But consider the following as a better model. Since our vastly expanding armaments industries create in whole sections and in millions of workers a vested economic interest in war, a bill was introduced in Congress–I think by Kastenmeier[101] of Wisconsin–to require armaments manufacturers to prepare plans for alternative peaceful use of the expanded plant as a condition for getting an armaments contract. On this model I have suggested a proposal, that might be applicable in Canada: to countervail the brain-washing inevitable with the vast audiences of mass-media controlled by a few centers, impose a small progressive tax on audience size–a tax for revenue, not to prohibit–to underwrite independent media with rival views. By the same reasoning, corporations that greatly improve their position by technological advances, e.g. automation, have a responsibility to provide relevant education of the young, whose entry into society is made more difficult. At present, of course, these corporations do just the opposite: they urge the public and parents to spend money to train A algebrists whom they will use, after national examinations have weeded out the B's and C's. And they have even managed to get the public to pay for training their semi-skilled workers, by taking over the job camps of the poverty program.

The advantage of proposals like these is that they consti-tutionally guarantee countervalance whenever a group begins to have a great influence: the danger generates its own antidote, without punitive machinery which has no positive result and without adding new levels of regulation and administration.

A major means of creating an effective pluralism is decentrali-zation, to increase the amount of mind and the number of wills initiating and deciding. Very many functions of modern society must, of course, be centralized, and in my opinion there are many other functions which should be more centralized than they are now. (I

---

[101] Robert William Kastenmeier (Born 1924) represented Wisconsin in the United States House of Representatives from 1959 to 1991, and is a member of the Democratic Party.

have discussed this question in a book called *People or Personnel.*) On the whole, however, we would be wise at present to decentralize wherever it is feasible without too great loss of efficiency. Indeed, in a wide range of enterprises, decentralization means a gain in efficiency.

The current style is the opposite: big corporations invade new fields in which they have no competence, just to get contracts, and they will not easily be persuaded to change. Yet a lot could be done by public policy, e.g. to give out public money preferably to small independent firms in Research and Development, urban planning and renewal, and communications. At present, farm subsidies favor big plantations and chain-grocers; they could often as well or better favor smaller farmers and co-operatives. In schooling, a case can be made for the consolidation of rural schools, but there is no doubt that urban systems should be radically decentralized. Many giant universities would have more vitality, and be cheaper to run, if they were allowed to fall apart into their natural faculties and schools. It is indispensable for social work to be administered locally and democratically in order to combat anomie. Neighborhood treatment of mental diseases seems to make sense in most cases. The experience of the Peckham Health Center[102] in London suggests that it is better for many other parts of medicine. And, as I argued in a previous lecture, many urban problems that are prohibitively expensive and intractable in the city could be better handled in the depopulating countryside and be a grounds for rural reconstruction.

A chief reason to encourage decentralism is just to have a countervailing style of enterprise, one that does not require big capital, grandiose overhead, and all kinds of connections and

---

[102] The Peckham Experiment took place between 1926 and 1950, initially generated by rising public concern over the health of the working class and an increasing interest in preventative social medicine. George Scott Williamson (1884-1953) and Innes Hope Pearse (1889-1978), a husband and wife team, opened the Pioneer Health Centre in a working class area of Peckham.

credentials. The liberal sociologists of pluralism don't understand the matter of style, but many conservatives understand it very well and therefore have much in common with the new radicals. The older "planning" radicalism of the Thirties, however, played right into the present liberal social engineering.

5

To conclude this series of lectures on the crisis of the American political experiment, populist, pluralist, libertarian, let me say something about our peculiar American libertarianism, which is, I guess,–along with our energy and enterprise–what most impresses Europeans about us. As a theme of history, the American kind of freedom has been traced to many things: the Americans were Englishmen, they were yeomen, they were Protestant refugees, they were other refugees, they had an open frontier–all these are relevant. But I am struck also by a constitutional aspect which I like, perhaps, to exaggerate.

Of all politically advanced peoples, the Americans are the only ones who started in an historical golden age of Anarchy. Having gotten rid of the King–and he was always far away, as well as being only an English king–they were in no hurry to reconstruct another sovereign, or even a concept of sovereignty. For more than thirty years after the outbreak of the Revolution, almost nobody bothered to vote in formal elections (often less than 2%), and the national Constitution was the concern of a few merchants and lawyers. Yet the Americans were not a primitive or unpolitical people; on the contrary they had many kinds of civilized democratic and hierarchical structures: town meetings, congregational parishes, masters with apprentices and indentured servants, gentry with slaves, professionals and clients, provincial assemblies. The pluralism goes way back. But where was the sovereignty?

Theoretically, the sovereignty resided in the People. But except for sporadic waves of protest, like the riots, Tea Parties, and the Revolutionary War itself—the populism also goes way back—who were the People? One does not at all have the impression, in this congeries of families, face to face communities, and pluralist social relations, that there was anything like a General Will,[103] except maybe to be let alone.

Nevertheless, there is—it is clear from American behavior—a characteristic kind of sovereignty. It is what is made up by political people as they go along, a continuous series of existential constitutional acts, just as they invented the Declaration, the Articles, and the Constitution, and obviously expected to keep re-writing the Constitution. The founding fathers were saddled with a Roman language, so they spoke of "inalienable rights"; but the American theory is idiomatically expressed by pragmatists like William James: I have certain rights and will act accordingly, including finally punching you in the nose if you don't concede them.

I was recently vividly reminded of the American idea of sovereignty when there were some sit-ins at the City Hall in Detroit and the Governor of Michigan said, in a voice that could only be called plaintive, "There is no Black Power, there is no White Power, there is no Mixed Power; the only power belongs to the government"—I presume that his textbook had said, "The only power belongs to the State." But there was no mystique in the Governor's textbook proposition; I doubt if anybody, but anybody, took it seriously as an assertion of moral authority, or as anything but a threat to call the cops. On the question of sovereignty, the unmistakable undertone in these incidents is, "Well, that remains to be seen."

---

[103] The general will, made famous by Jean-Jacques Rousseau, is a concept in political philosophy referring to will of a people as a whole. As used by Rousseau, the "general will" is identical to the rule of law.

6

In the context of this pragmatic American attitude toward sovereignty, what is the meaning of the present wave of civil disobedience? Against direct actions like the civil rights sit-ins, the student occupation of Sproul Hall[104] at Berkeley, the draft-card burnings, it is always said that they foment disrespect for law and order and lead to a general breakdown of civil society. Although judicious people are willing to grant that due process and ordinary administration are not working well, because of prejudice, unconcern, doubletalk, arrogance, or perhaps just the cumbersomeness of overcentralized bureaucracy, nevertheless, they say, the recourse to civil disobedience entails even worse evils.

This is an apparently powerful argument. Even those who engage in civil disobedience tend to concede it, but, they say, in a crisis they cannot act otherwise; they are swept by indignation, or they are morally compelled to resist evil. Or, as I mentioned in my last lecture, they have an apocalyptic theory in which they are acting for a "higher" justice, and the present order is no longer legitimate.

In my opinion, all these views are exaggerations because they assign a status and finality to the sovereign which in America it does not have. If the State is not quite so determinate, then the insult to it does not necessarily have such global consequences. Certainly the American genius, whether we cite Jefferson or James and Dewey more than a century later, is that the State is in process, in a kind of regulated permanent revolution.

Empirically, is it the case that direct actions which are aimed at specific abuses lead to general lawlessness? Where is the evidence to prove the connection, e.g. statistics of correlative disorder in the

---

[104] See note 38.

community, or an increase of unspecific lawless acts among the direct activists? The flimsy evidence that there is tends to weigh in the opposite direction. Crime and delinquency seem to diminish where there has been political direct action by black Americans. The community and academic spirit at Berkeley has been better this year than it used to be. In 1944 the warden of Danbury prison[105] assured me that the war-objectors penned up there were, in general, "the finest type of citizens!"

On sociological grounds, indeed the probability is that a specific direct action, that cuts through frustrating due process, and especially if it is successful or partially successful, will tend to increase civil order rather than to destroy it, for it revives the belief that the community is one's own, that one has influence; whereas the inhibition of direct action against an intolerable abuse inevitably increases anomie and therefore *general* lawlessness. The enforcement of law and order at all costs aggravates the tensions that lead to explosions. But if place is allowed for "creative disorder," as Arthur Waskow[106] calls it, there is less tension, less resignation, and more likelihood of finding social, economic, and political expedients to continue with.

Of course, this raises a nice legal question: how to distinguish between a rioting mob and citizens engaging in creative disorder? Theoretically, it is a rioting mob, according to the wisdom of LeBon[107] and Freud, if it is in the grip of unconscious ideas of Father or the need to destroy Father, if it is after senseless power or to

---

[105] Danbury, Connecticut, 3 miles north of downtown Danbury and 70 miles from New York City. This prison was known popularly as a "country club" prison, especially among mobsters who were sent here.

[106] Arthur Ocean Waskow (born 1933) is an American author, political activist, and rabbi. Waskow was arrested many times for protests against racial segregation, the Vietnam War, the Soviet Union's oppression of Jews, South African apartheid, and the Iraq war.

[107] Gustave Le Bon (1841–1931) was a French social psychologist, sociologist, and amateur physicist. His work on crowd psychology became important during the first half of the twentieth century when it was used by media researchers such as Hadley Cantril and Herbert Blumer to describe the reactions of subordinate groups to media.

destroy senseless power. Perhaps it is a group of confused Americans if it is demanding to be paid attention to, and included, as the first step of political thinking. Perhaps it is petitioning for a redress of grievances, even if it has no writ of grievances to present, and even if there is no sovereign to petition. In any case, the part of wisdom is to take people seriously and come up with a new idea that might make a difference to their problems. If the governors won't, or can't, do this, then we must do it. I am often asked by radical students what I am trying to do with all my utopian thinking and inventing of alternatives; perhaps the use of intellect is to help turn riot into creative disorder.

In brief, contrary to the conventional argument, anarchic incidents like civil disobedience are often essential parts of the democratic process as Americans understand it. So it was understood by Jefferson when, after Shays's rebellion[108] was disarmed, he urged that nobody be punished, for that might discourage mutiny in the future, and then what check would there be on government? So, in milder terms, it has been recently understood by the pragmatic Court, where many cases of apparently obvious trespass and violation have turned out to be legal after all, and only subsequently made legal by statute. This is not, I believe, because the Court has been terrorized or has blinked in order to avoid worse evils, but because in rapidly changing circumstances, there is often no other way to know what the Constitution is.

7

Finally, I need hardly point out that in American rhetoric, American freedom—in an anarchic sense—has been held to be the

---

[108] Shays' Rebellion was an armed uprising in central and western Massachusetts (mainly Springfield) from 1786 to 1787. The rebellion is named after Daniel Shays, a veteran of the American Revolutionary War. The rebellion started on August 21, 1786, over financial difficulties and by January 1787, over one thousand Shaysites had been arrested.

philosopher's stone of our famous energy and enterprise. Mossback conservatives have always spoken for laissez-faire as the right climate for economic progress (though, to be sure, they then connive for tariffs and subsidies, hire strikebreakers, and form monopolies in restraint of trade). Radical liberals have cleaved to the Bill of Rights, for to be cowed by authority makes it impossible to think and experiment. Immigrants used to flock to the United States to avoid conscription, as some of our best youth now go to Canada. They came because there were no class barriers, and because there was open opportunity to make good in one's own way. And every American kid soon learns to say, "It's a free country—you can't make me!"

By and large, let me say, this rhetoric has been true. Anarchism is grounded in a rather definite social-psychological hypothesis: that forceful, graceful, and intelligent behavior occurs only when there is an uncoerced and direct response to the environment; that in most human affairs, more harm than good results from compulsion, top-down direction, bureaucratic planning, pre-ordained curricula, jails, conscription, States. Sometimes it is necessary to limit freedom, as we keep a child from running across the highway, but this is usually at the expense of force, grace, and learning; and in the long run it is usually wiser to remove the danger and simplify the rules than to hamper the activity. I think, I say, that this hypothesis is true, but whether or not it is, it would certainly be un-American to deny it. Everybody knows that America is great because America is free; and by freedom is not finally meant the juridical freedom of the European tradition, freedom under law, having the legal rights and duties of citizens; what is meant is the spontaneous freedom of anarchy, opportunity to do what you can, although hampered by necessary conventions, as few as possible.

Then, how profoundly alien our present establishment is!—that has in one generation crept up on us and occupied all the positions of power. It has been largely the product of war, of the dislocations after World War I, the crash programs of World War II, and going on for twenty years the chronic low-grade emergency of the Cold War. It is fanning again into war.

The term "establishment" itself is borrowed from the British—for snobbish and literary reasons, and usually with an edge of satire. But we have had no sovereign to establish such a thing, and there is no public psychology to accept it as legitimate. It operates like an establishment: it is the consensus of politics, the universities and science, big business, organized labor, public schooling, the media of communications, the official language; it determines the right style and accredits its own members; it hires and excludes, subsidizes and neglects. But it has no warrant of legitimacy, it has no tradition, it cannot talk straight English, it neither has produced nor could produce any art, it does not lead by moral means but by a kind of social engineering, and it is held in contempt and detestation by the young. The American tradition—I think the *abiding* American tradition—is pluralist, populist, and libertarian, while the establishment is monolithic, mandarin, and managed. Its only claim, that it is efficient, is false. It is fantastically wasteful of brains, money, the environment, and people. It is channeling our energy and enterprise to its own aggrandizement and power, and it will exhaust us.

I would almost say that my country is like a conquered province with foreign rulers, except that they are not foreigners and we are responsible for what they do.

8

Let me assess our situation as soberly as I can. The system at present dominant in America will not do, it is too empty. On the other hand, it is possible that classical American democracy is necessarily a thing of the past; it may be too wild, too woolly, too mixed—too anarchic, too populist, too pluralist—for the conditions of big population and high technology in a world that has become small. I hope not, for I love the American experiment, but I don't know.

We Americans have not suffered as most other peoples have, at least not since the Civil War a century ago. We have not been bombed, we have not been occupied. We have not cringed under a real tyranny. Perhaps we would not ride so high today if we knew what it felt like to be badly hurt.

The American faces that used to be so beautiful, so resolute and yet poignantly open and innocent, are looking ugly these days, hard, thin-lipped, and like innocence spoilt without having become experienced. For our sake, as well as your own, be wary of us.